General editor: Graham Handley

Brodie's Notes on Thomas Hardy's

Far from the Madding Crowd

I. L. Baker BA

Pan Books London, Sydney and Auckland

First published by James Brodie Ltd

This edition first published 1976 by Pan Books Ltd

Revised 1991 by
Pan Books Ltd, Cavaye Place, London SW10 9PG

9 8 7 6 5 4 3 2 1

© I. L. Baker 1976

ISBN 0 330 50312 X

Photoset by Parker Typesetting Service, Leicester

Printed and bound in Great Britain by
Clays Ltd, St Ives plc, Bungay, Suffolk

Contents

Page references in these Notes are to the Pan
edition of *Far from the Madding Crowd* but references
are also given to particular chapters, so that
the Notes may be used with any edition of the novel.

Preface

The intention throughout this study aid is to stimulate and guide, to encourage your involvement in the book, and to develop informed responses and a sure understanding of the main details.

Brodie's Notes provide a clear outline of the play or novel's plot, followed by act, scene, or chapter summaries and/or commentaries. These are designed to emphasize the most important literary and factual details. Poems, stories or non-fiction texts combine brief summary with critical commentary on individual aspects or common features of the genre being examined. Textual notes define what is difficult or obscure and emphasize literary qualities. Revision questions are set at appropriate points to test your ability to appreciate the prescribed book and to write accurately and relevantly about it.

In addition, each of these Notes includes a critical appreciation of the author's art. This covers such major elements as characterization, style, structure, setting and themes. Poems are examined technically – rhyme, rhythm, for instance. In fact, any important aspect of the prescribed work will be evaluated. The aim is to send you back to the text you are studying.

Each study aid concludes with a series of general questions which require a detailed knowledge of the book: some of these questions may invite comparison with other books, some will be suitable for coursework exercises, and some could be adapted to work you are doing on another book or books. Each study aid has been adapted to meet the needs of the current examination requirements. They provide a basic, individual and imaginative response to the work being studied, and it is hoped that they will stimulate you to acquire disciplined reading habits and critical fluency.

Graham Handley 1990

The author and his work

Thomas Hardy was born on 2 June 1840, in a brick and thatch house in the hamlet of Upper Bockhampton, in the parish of Stinsford, near Dorchester in Dorset. Hardy, like his father before him, spent the major part of his life in this area. Hardy's father, a buoyant and kindly man, was a master mason (or builder); quite well-to-do but unambitious, and devoted to music, for Hardys had played and sung the music for the Stinsford Parish Church for over a hundred years. Hardy inherited this passionate interest in music: he could tune a fiddle as a lad, play it as a youth at weddings and festivals; and he would join in the dancing, often weeping with emotion. He was extremely sensitive to music all his life, and he long remembered the tunes of his childhood. His mother (and her mother, too) was an omnivorous reader, and cast in a heroic mould. 'She was of the stuff of which great men's mothers are made', is said of Bathsheba (Chapter 54, p.377), but it could well have applied to, and may even be a recollection of, his own mother.

Hardy was a delicate child (he had to be resuscitated at birth) and had no formal schooling until he was eight: but his mental precocity, the atmosphere of books and music, and the rich well-watered countryside around sufficiently fed his imagination. Besides, like his father, he was completely unambitious, and had no wish to grow up. Eventually the village school at Lower Bockhampton claimed him, and his reading extended to such material as Dryden's *Virgil* and Johnson's *Rasselas*. A year later Hardy entered the Dorchester day school where, at fourteen, he won a first prize for diligence.

Hardy had started Latin at the age of twelve, and then read his Virgil in the original: he also devoured the works of Shakespeare, Scott, Dumas, Milton and sundry popular novelists of the day. He had extra lessons in French and German, and taught at Sunday School, learning off the services and much of the Bible by heart. Hardy was popular at school, though he remained essentially aloof, and a lover of solitude. He was fastidious, never bearing anyone to touch him; and already, reinforced by his classical reading and the sight of some public hangings, had a stark view of the tragedy and the injustices of human life.

At the age of twenty Hardy went into the offices of an ecclesiastical architect in Dorchester; his master, John Hicks, was an educated man, and a competent classical scholar. Hardy usually rose early to study his Latin (often at 4 a.m. in the summer), and learned Greek on his own: his already marked intellectual precocity flourished and blossomed with contacts such as his master, a near neighbour William Barnes (a dialect poet and philosopher), other scholarly acquaintances, and fine craftsmen.

In 1862 Hardy was in London, still working as an architect and restorer, but widening his reading and artistic bent in the cultural wealth of the capital. He visited its museums, galleries and libraries: he studied painting, being particularly interested in light and shade effects. He read deeply and widely in all manner of subjects, particularly in science and philosophy. The works of Darwin, Huxley, J. S. Mill and Herbert Spencer, whose unorthodoxy in various fields had an immense influence in liberating thought from traditionally accepted beliefs, had a profound effect on the young Hardy: by the age of thirty he was intellectually an agnostic.

More practically, however, Hardy had to decide, despite his inherent lack of ambition, what to do for his livelihood. He considered art criticism, even the Church, play-writing, and architecture, for which he had been long trained and at which he was undoubtedly competent. In 1867 Hardy returned to Dorchester as an assistant to his old principal, Mr Hicks. It was now, back at home, that he started to write fiction. His first effort, *The Poor Man and the Lady* was rejected by the publishing house of Macmillan. In 1871 another attempt, *Desperate Remedies*, was accepted only at his own risk by a lesser-known firm. This made little impact, yet despite its experimental nature it bears what we now recognize as the Hardy stamp, with its rather morbid episodes, its church and churchyard scenes, a certain air of fantasy, and some emotional force. All of these were intensified and improved in his next novels, *Under The Greenwood Tree*, an idyll of the Wessex scene, and *A Pair of Blue Eyes* (1873), much more ambitious and verbally skilful.

During this time Hardy had met Emma Gifford while doing architectural work on a church Hicks had been instructed to restore. Emma was a devotedly religious, rather solitary, yet vital and graceful woman; they married in September 1874 on the strength of Hardy's next novel, *Far from the Madding Crowd*, which appeared in the illustrious *Cornhill* magazine from January to November 1874, an immediate success both as a serial and as a complete volume. His new wife encouraged Hardy to stick to writing, which he did, caring little for the consequent fame, wealth, social success and indeed hostility which now came his way.

Thereafter, until the age of fifty-eight, Hardy wrote a further ten novels, some short stories, and a play: during this period, after having moved about at home and abroad, he finally settled down at a house called Max Gate, of his own design, in Dorchester. He had achieved fame and security; his circle of eminent friends had widened enormously. The novels, many pitiless and tragic in theme, often shocked Victorian sentiments and taste; Hardy made little concession to this, exposing relentlessly his view of the tragic and insoluble problems of human existence for which religion offered no solution. It was a negative, resigned attitude that disturbed many.

In 1898 Hardy abruptly turned his back upon the novel, utterly and completely, returning to his first and strongest love of poetry with his collection of *Wessex Poems*. Personal domestic tragedy clouded his life at this period: Hardy's and his wife's opposite dispositions and characters had eventually brought them to lead separate lives. The marriage had been childless, much to Hardy's sorrow; religious differences had become more sensitively acute; and Hardy's complete lack of social ambition all seem to have culminated in a distressing emotional disturbance for his wife, with apparent tendency towards delusions, leading to Emma's death, for which Hardy, in some poignant verse, felt partly responsible.

Two years later in 1914, he married an old friend of the family, who had been his secretary and was herself a writer; and Florence Dugdale, who later wrote an indispensable biography of her husband, made happy the remaining years by her humour, sympathy and critical understanding.

Sensitive lyrical poetry, of exquisite concentration and feeling, now flowed: the greatest living novelist was hailed as a significant poet: and some critics believe that posterity will rate Hardy's poetry more highly than his novels. Honours were showered on this quiet, yet sprightly, charming and vigorously intellectual man, especially after the publication of *The Dynasts*, a verse-drama of the Napoleonic Wars, a unique philosophic history and epic drama. Five universities (Scottish and English) conferred honorary degrees on one who had never been formally taught beyond the grammar school; he received the Order of Merit in 1910, and the Gold Medal of the Royal Society of Literature in 1911; but his greatest pleasure came with his award of the Freedom of Dorchester. His works were constantly reprinted, and he left a fortune of nearly £100,000. He died on 11 January 1928.

The irony which pervades much of his work was given a dramatic twist after his death. It was decided that the man who never sought fame should be buried in Westminster Abbey: there were quarrels over precedence for tickets, and the Prime Minister was among the illustrious who bore the pall. The avowed agnostic was buried in England's national shrine. The body was cremated, and the ashes interred in Poets' Corner, next to Dickens's grave, with a spadeful of Dorset earth thrown over. But his heart was carried back to Stinsford, and was buried in the grave of his first wife.

Title and sources of names

Title

Far from the Madding Crowd was Hardy's fourth novel, but only the second to be published under his own name. Already one notes the allusive and ironic nature of his choice of title, a device which he often used later. The inescapable and obvious reference is to Thomas Gray's celebrated *Elegy written in a Country Churchyard* (stanza nineteen):

Far from the madding crowd's ignoble strife,
  Their sober wishes never learn'd to stray;
Along the cool sequester'd vale of life
  They kept the noiseless tenour of their way.

At first glance Gray and Hardy could be talking of similar rural communities, barely altered as they were in many ways over the intervening years: the small closely-knit farming communities, rarely moving from their hamlets and villages, with a strong sense of agricultural and historical continuity (see especially Chapter 22), where town life (of discreet Bath!) is a source of gaping bewilderment. The resemblances, however, are superficial. Even the village is changing, and we can see from Chapter 8 that the 'old times' are looked back upon with affection, and the new with some suspicion.

Intruders arrive, such as Bathsheba and Troy, breaking up some of the calm and peace: the consequences include broken hearts, seduction, pitiful death, insanity, murder, and a life sentence. The 'ignoble strife' is here, right in Weatherbury itself, transferred temporarily from the materialistic world outside, and forming the basis of the story. It is superimposed upon a village and its people who were by no means perfect or idyllic, or particularly 'cool' or noiseless in their everyday relationships. We are not so far from the 'madding crowd' after all; and this miniature, yet universal, battle of emotions is played out between a pastoral opening and close. The title is part and parcel of Hardy's view of human endeavour in an unfeeling universe.

Sources of names

A brief comment on the names. It is not of course essential for an author to use names in any way indicative of some trait or characteristic: but skilful naming (as regularly practised by Dickens, for example) can help to form an atmosphere appropriate to conditions and setting. Hardy was a well-read, educated man who knew his classics and Bible thoroughly. He also knew the people and the places he was writing about in considerable detail from personal involvement and contact. Thus he is realistic in his choice of names. In the comparatively stable and rather static agricultural communities of his day (and of course before then too) most Christian names would be derived from the Bible. Surnames as such, indeed, were almost unknown among the mass of the people before the Norman Conquest. When they did evolve in the succeeding four centuries or so, they were generally based on occupation, nickname, or the local habitation of the bearer or his family.

So far as the Christian names of the characters in *Far from the Madding Crowd* are concerned they run true to expectation: Gabriel, Joseph, Mark, Laban, Benjamin, Matthew, Andrew among the men, and, of course, Bathsheba among the women. It would not be reasonable to lay too much stress on the Biblical stories associated with these names: but, for those who know their Bible, Bathsheba is particularly remembered as the wife of Uriah the Hittite (2 Samuel, xi and xii; 1 Kings, i and ii), with whom David committed adultery, having her husband killed, the better to effect his purpose: and Gabriel (Hebrew for 'Man of God') is one of the archangels. Something perhaps of these associations has some relevance to the characters of the story.

Of the exceptions, that is the non-Biblical first names, it is interesting to note that William (Boldwood) is Germanic in origin, meaning 'a resolute protector'; and that both Frank (Troy) and Fanny (Robin) are derived from the same root, from Francis, again with religious overtones. And Troy, who appears superficially to be the most frank and candid of all, is in many ways the only liar of the story.

The surnames are mainly local and agricultural. Everdene explains itself, as the 'dene' suffix indicates a small valley; Boldwood too is obviously rural, as are Poorgrass, Smallbury ('bury' meaning a town), and Warren. Troy may well be a deliberate twist of Hardy's Roy-Town, which exists in fact as Troy-Town; Ball is a common field name in Somerset and is also recorded as a nickname for 'bald', and Randle is an old Anglo-Saxon name.

There is no need to explore this further: Hardy clearly used familiar appropriate names, some no doubt with a hint of deeper association, but most merely in keeping with the commonplace and expected names of the countryfolk among whom he had lived and whose history and traditions he wished to immortalize, for he held them dear.

Chapter summaries, textual notes and revision questions

Chapter 1

Farmer Gabriel Oak of Norcombe, a young bachelor of sensible character and admirable physique, observes, without her knowing, a beautiful but rather vain girl moving into the district with all her belongings on a waggon. She quibbles over paying twopence at the toll-gate, and Oak pays for her, for which he receives no thanks.

Laodicean neutrality Indifference to religion. See Revelation, iii, 14–18.

Nicene creed The Creed, formulated at the great Council of Nicaea (AD 325), used in the Holy Communion Service of the Church of England, and in other ritual.

a coat like Dr Johnson's The great lexicographer and critic (1709–84) often wore, according to his celebrated biographer James Boswell, a large brown cloth greatcoat with voluminous pockets.

Norcombe Hill One of the hills in the neighbourhood of Eggardon, between Dorchester and Bridport.

geraniums, myrtles, and cactuses Not all these may be familiar. Myrtles are evergreen shrubs with shining oval leaves, fragrant white flowers, and aromatic purple berries; geraniums are mostly small plants with small regular flowers and divided leaves, with a pungent odour: English garden geraniums are, in fact, usually of another species; and the cactus family are fleshy, thickened and usually spiny plants. No mention is given of which of many varieties are here seen, nor is it important.

turnpike-gate Gate across a road to prevent the passage of vehicles or pedestrians until a toll is paid.

St John This could refer either to St John, whose mother was sister to Mary, the mother of Christ, or to John the Baptist, the last of the Old Testament prophets. Either could well be portrayed in the stained-glass windows of the village church.

Judas Iscariot The disciple who betrayed Christ, his Master, for thirty pieces of silver. The story is told in all the Gospels.

Chapter 2

Gabriel Oak, an ex-bailiff and once a shepherd, is now, by his own efforts a sheep-farmer on his own account. At midnight the notes of his flute sound clearly through the imposing starlit night on Norcombe Hill from his movable shepherd's hut. Later he moves about his flock, rescuing and reviving a new-born lamb: as he returns it to the mother he notices a distant light. He walks towards it, and through a hole in the hut from which it came he sees two women busy in nursing a cow and her new-born calf: the young girl is the same one who Oak saw enter the village, and for whom he paid the toll. The elder woman is her aunt Mrs Hurst with whom she is staying.

St Thomas's St Thomas was the Apostle who doubted (see John, xxi,25): his feast day is 21 December.

Toller-Down The name of an actual down in Dorset.

in the wind's eye Directly opposed to the wind.

the Bear The Great Bear, or Ursa Major. This is one of the northern constellations, its brightest stars forming the Plough or Charles's Wain.

Sirius The brightest star in the sky, also called Alpha Canis Majoris, or Dog-star.

Capella One of the three brightest stars in the northern sky: the light is about 130 times as great as that of the sun.

Aldebaran A reddish-coloured star in the Hyades group, near the Pleiades, on which see note below.

Betelgueux The brightest star in the constellation of Orion, on which see note below.

Noah's Ark For the story of this Old Testament patriarch, the Flood and the Ark, see Genesis, viii,4.

turpentine A resinous oil obtained from various species of pine trees: in various forms it is used as a paint solvent and in medicine.

magnesia Oxide of magnesium (MgO): it is used in fire brick manufacture, and in medicine as a laxative.

ginger A herb native to the East Indies: it is used chiefly as a spice, but has some value in stomachic medicine.

castor-oil An oil pressed from the seeds of an Indian plant: it has various medicinal uses, principally as a purgative.

Dog-star See note on 'Sirius', above.

Pleiades A group of conspicuous stars marking the shoulder of the constellation of Taurus: to the eye only six stars are usually visible, but astronomical telescopes reveal over two thousand in a great cluster.

Orion One of the constellations, among the brightest in the sky, lying on the celestial equator south-east of Taurus.

Castor and Pollux The two stars marking the heads of the Heavenly Twins, in the constellation of Gemini.

Square of Pegasus A constellation easily recognizable by four stars marking out a great square: Alpha, Beta and Gamma Pegasi, and Alpha Andromedae.

Vega The second brightest star of the northern hemisphere: it is the first star, Alpha, Lyrae, in the constellation of the Lyre, with a brilliancy equal to that of fifty suns.

Cassiopeia's chair A constellation in the northern hemisphere, recognizable in shape as a lady on the throne, her five principal stars making a sprawling W outline.

bran-mash Preparation of boiled grain husks given warm to cattle as food.

Milton's Satan The proud Lucifer of Milton's *Paradise Lost*.

Lucina In Roman mythology, the goddess of childbirth, sometimes associated with Juno or Diana.

Chapter 3

The next day Oak sees the girl returning to the cattle-shed, and he secretly watches with some surprise her rather unconventional and masculine handling of her horse, and notes her fine poise and pleasant features. They converse, each rather distantly and shyly. At the end of the same cold week Oak nearly suffocates in his little hut by falling asleep without having first opened a ventilating slide. He wakes up to find his head on the girl's lap. Hearing the howling of Oak's dog, she has entered the hut to find a near-unconscious Farmer Oak, whom she has revived. Gabriel thanks her sincerely; they shake hands. Teasingly she insists on Gabriel's discovering her name, for she will not tell him.

Tewnell Mill Near Norcombe.

eight heads In classical art the head was taken as a unit of measurement; the whole body, in proper proportion, should be eight heads in length.

Nymphean Pertaining to nymphs, who were, in classical mythology, maidenly nature spirits who presided over some particular river, wood, mountain or sea: hence, by extension, the term would apply to any sprightly, handsome, graceful young girl.

Maiden's Blush ... Crimson Tuscany Varieties of rose, in increasing order of scarlet intensity of colour.

contretemps Unexpected accident which throws everything into confusion.

Samson For the story of the Biblical hero of miraculous strength see Judges, xiii–xii, 31.

Chapter 4

Gabriel discovers that the girl's name is Bathsheba Everdene: he feels that he loves her, and resolves to make her his wife. He has thus to see her at her aunt's, for the visits to the cowshed, constantly watched unobserved by Gabriel, have now ceased. He finds, or takes, an opportunity in taking a lamb to the aunt, Mrs Hurst, after dressing himself unusually meticulously. The girl is out; but Mrs Hurst, to whom Gabriel reveals his intentions, indicates that Bathsheba is so good-looking and talented that she can choose a husband from many possible suitors. At this Gabriel leaves, but he is called back by Bathsheba running after him. A long conversation follows about marriage, and Bathsheba eventually says that as she does not love Gabriel, she cannot marry him; Gabriel, for himself, insists that his feelings will never change. Upon her suggesting that such a marriage would be ridiculous, Gabriel ruefully tells her that he will never ask again.

'Full . . . nothing' The quotation is from Shakespeare's *Macbeth*, V,5,27–8.

whiting A preparation of finely powdered chalk used for cleaning plate and other metallic surfaces.

guano A natural manure found in great abundance on some sea coasts, especially on the islands about Peru, consisting of the excrement of sea-fowl; it is chalky-white in colour generally.

Roman cement A cement or hydraulic mortar made by the addition of chalky or clayey matter to lime, sand and water.

mace A spice consisting of the dried outer covering of the nutmeg.

frame A low glass-topped box-like container, placed over the soil, for 'forcing' delicate or difficult plants.

Ecclesiastes A book of the Old Testament. In tone, it is a mixture of despair and pessimism, yet with an irresistible sense of the goodness of God.

Chapter 5

Some time passes, and Bathsheba is known to have moved to Weatherbury, some 20 miles (32 km) away. Gabriel still loves her. One night, after tending his sheep as usual, Gabriel returns to his house with only one of his sheepdogs, the elder called George. The younger remains afield. Just before dawn the shepherd hears an unusual ringing of the sheep-bells, caused by the sheep running at great speed. He rushes out, and discovers, to his horror, that the young dog had run after the sheep, chasing them over a hill into a chalkpit, and two hundred uninsured ewes, many of them with lamb, lie at the bottom dead or dying.

Oak is now bankrupt, thankful only that he is not a married man in these circumstances. The dog is shot; Gabriel pays off his debts and is left with only the clothes he has on his back.

Weatherbury Puddletown; at times in the novel it is called Lower Longpuddle; most of the action of this story takes place here.

Turner's pictures The British painter Joseph Mallord William Turner (1775–1851) was notable for his vivid and moving colour effects, often of great romantic turbulence in their mass and variation. His later works foreshadowed Impressionism in their suggestive effects of glowing and brilliant colouring.

Hylas In Greek mythology Hylas was a handsome youth, beloved of Hercules. He went ashore to draw water on the coast of Mysia (a district of the north-west corner of Asia Minor) and was carried off by nymphs. Hercules long sought for him in vain.

Napoleon at St Helena The great Napoleon Bonaparte (1769–1821) was imprisoned on the island of St Helena by the British soon after the Battle of Waterloo (1815).

Revision questions on Chapters 1–5

1 Describe Oak's physical appearance and his character, as so far indicated.

2 What are the dominant impressions so far given of Bathsheba Everdene?

3 What exactly is Oak doing, and what are the two women doing, on or near Norcombe Hill?

4 Describe the circumstances of Bathsheba's entry into Gabriel's shepherd's hut, and give the gist of their subsequent conversation.

5 How did Oak prepare himself for the visit to Mrs Hurst?

6 How did Oak lose his sheep? What were his first, and then his later, thoughts on this misfortune?

Chapter 6

Two months later, at the Casterbridge hiring fair, Gabriel Oak, having at first tried and failed to secure a post as a bailiff, tries again as a shepherd: his honesty in declaring that he once owned a farm prevents his being taken on. At dusk, still unemployed, he earns some money with his flute playing.

Gabriel Oak decides to walk to Weatherbury, where Bathsheba had been bound some time ago: he enjoys an unexpected rest, and then a ride, in a cart, whose drivers talk about a vain girl who might well have been Bathsheba herself. Gabriel slips off, and then sees a fire, about half a mile away. Running into the blazing rickyard, he organizes the fire-fighting and does the most to smother the flames; he is soon aware that the successful mistress of the farm is indeed Bathsheba, who has lately taken over a dead uncle's estate. He asks for a job as shepherd.

Casterbridge Hardy's name for Dorchester: it features in twelve of his works, and in this novel at least sixteen localities of the town are mentioned. Dorchester itself is an old town of Dorset, the Durnovaria of the Romans, with many British and Roman antiquities.

Siddim See Genesis, xiv,3–10.

'Jockey to the Fair' A popular favourite, in great vogue about 1780 (though it was composed before then), by A. Moffat and F. Kidson.

Arcadian Of Arcadia, a country in the centre of the Peloponnesus, whose people claimed to be the most ancient in Greece: hence, by extension, the term is used to denote an extreme pastoral or rustic atmosphere.

Shottsford Hardy's name for Blandford, or Blandford Forum, a market town of Dorset, on the river Stour, some 16 miles (25 km) north-east of Dorchester.

Charles's Wain An old popular name for the Great Bear constellation, for which see note p.15.

dandy cattle Dialect term for fine (flashy, showy) folk.

lucifer See note on 'Milton's Satan', p.16. (The term was also used for an early type of striking match.)

rick-yard The part of a farmyard where the ricks, or stacks of hay, are erected.

'reed-drawing' Combing out rough straw.

pitch-and-toss sovereign Pitch and toss is a game in which coins are thrown at a mark, the player throwing nearest having the right of tossing all, and keeping those that come down heads up: the obvious implication is that he was very rich.

Chapter 7

Bathsheba recognizes Oak; she asks him to settle his new position with her bailiff, a rather unsociable man called Pennyways. Oak makes his way to Warren's Malthouse, where he can expect to get some food and temporary lodging: on his way there he meets a slight young girl who ask him to keep his knowledge of her whereabouts secret. Oak agrees, and gives her a shilling, which is gratefully accepted. Oak moves off into Weatherbury to find the inn.

Ashtoreth The goddess of love, beauty and fertility among the Canaanites and Phoenicians, called Ishtar by the Babylonians, Aphrodite by the Greeks, and Venus by the Romans. The flavour here, however, is Biblical.

Warren's Malthouse A public house or tavern in Weatherbury, so called from its proprietor. It was the rendezvous of the local farmhands but has been pulled down many years since.

Buck's Head Inn An inn at Roy-Town (Hardy's name for Troy-Town) about 1 ½ miles (3 km) from Weatherbury. It was a famous inn in the old coaching days, but has now disappeared.

femoral artery The main blood vessel of the thigh.

Lower Longpuddle Strictly, this is Hardy's name (in another work) for Puddlehinton, a small village a little north of Weatherbury, but in this novel it is often used for Weatherbury itself.

Chapter 8

At Warren's Malthouse a group of village and farmworkers recognize Gabriel as the new shepherd: Gabriel has some welcome food and drink, learns more of Bathsheba's uncle and his sudden death, and of her father and mother. Gabriel is invited to play his flute, much to the company's enjoyment. Some men leave for their homes, but one rushes back with the news that Bathsheba's bailiff, Pennyways, has been caught red-handed stealing from his mistress, and has been discharged on the spot.

A moment later another villager enters with the news that Fanny Robin, Bathsheba's youngest servant-girl, is missing, and suicide is suspected: however, Bathsheba summons them to her house. There she asks some of them to make local enquiries about Fanny; a soldier friend is mentioned, and one man is despatched to the barracks to glean what information he can. Oak is taken to Coggan's home, one of the farmworkers, and there he dreams of future plans.

Elymas-the-Sorcerer The name of 'a certain Sorcerer, a false prophet', in Act, xiii,6–12; hence a trickster of half-mystical, half-scientific deceitful pretensions.

chinchilla The name of an animal, and its fur: the original is a genus of small rodents peculiar to South America, but the term is also used of a variety of rabbit bred for its fur.

use-money A dialect term for interest, as money paid for the use of money lent, or for the forbearance of a debt.

Saint-Simonian notions Socialist ideas, after Claude Henri, Comte de Saint-Simon (1760–1825), a French aristocrat, imprisoned during the Revolution, who yet sympathized with its principles. His doctrines enjoyed a wide vogue.

Greenhill A hill overlooking Kingsbere (Bere Regis): on the summit are the remains of an ancient earthwork known as Woodbury Camp. The hill encloses some 30 acres of level ground and was the scene of the annual fair which was held for a week from 18 September.

jerry-go-nimble Circus.

ba'dy Bawdy.

Yalbury Bottom A field at the foot of Yalbury Hill, or Yellowham Hill, 3 miles (5 km) from Dorchester.

Lambing-Down Gate Near Weatherbury.

Belief The Apostles' Creed, beginning 'I believe in God, the Father Almighty.'

lime-basket Wicker basket made waterproof by a coating of lime cement.

Buck's Head See note p.20.

White Monday Now called Whit Monday, the day after Whit Sunday.

long hundreds Six score: a hundred and twenty.

Let Your Light so Shine Usually part of the priestly benediction, based on Matthew, v,16.

charity-boy Orphan, maintained or supported by or in a charitable institution.

Durnover Durnover itself is Hardy's name for Fordington, a suburb of Dorchester, occupying the site of the old Roman town of Durnovaria. The Moor, mentioned later in Chapters 40 and 54, is Fordington Moor, near Dorchester.

Mellstock Hardy's name for an area near Dorchester on the east road to Puddletown, comprising the hamlets of Lewstock, the Bockhamptons, and Stinsford.

Candlemas Candlemas Day is 2 February, the Feast of the Purification of the Virgin Mary, when Christ was presented to her in the Temple. In Catholic churches all the candles which will be needed during the year are consecrated on this day.

'Dame Durden' This song enjoyed great popularity at Harvest Home and other festivals in the south of England.

Minerva In Roman mythology the goddess of wisdom and patroness of the arts and trades.

crowner's inquest Coroner's inquest, held in circumstances of death by other than natural causes.

The Young Man's Best Companion A bound volume of a magazine. Such 'uplifting' magazines were popular at the time.

The Farrier's Sure Guide By a William Gibson, published first in 1720, and running into seven editions.

The Veterinary Surgeon Probably *The Veterinary Surgeon, or Farriery taught on a new and simple Plan*, by John Hinds, 1827.

Paradise Lost Milton's great epic, published in twelve books in 1667.

The Pilgrim's Progress The celebrated allegory of the travels of Christian, by John Bunyan (1628–88).

Robinson Crusoe The celebrated romance by Daniel Defoe, published in 1719, describing the adventures fo the shipwrecked Crusoe and his Man Friday.

Ash's *Dictionary* This would appear to be that by John Ash, *The New and Complete Dictionary of the English Language*, published originally in 1775.

Walkingame's *Arithmetic* This is doubtless Francis Walkingame (about 1751–1785), an English educational writer: one of his arithmetic books, *The Tutor's Assistant*, was much used even up to the mid-nineteenth century.

Revision questions on Chapters 6–8

1 Explain the workings of chance or coincidence within these chapters: are they too far-fetched to be possible?

2 Describe Oak's actions at the hiring fair. Why was he not engaged?

3 How did Oak successfully organize the quelling of the fire?

4 Describe Bathsheba's reactions upon seeing Oak again.

5 Identify as many as you can of the frequenters of the malthouse: what information is there given about Bathsheba and her family, and about the life of the farmworkers?

6 Show how the two events which conclude 'The Chat' have in some way been hinted at in earlier chapters.

7 Chapter 8 is in fact the longest in the entire book. Can you give any reasons why this should be so, at such an early part of the story? To introduce us to the characters And setting which is to form the main plot in the book!

Chapter 9

In the old farmhouse Bathsheba and her personal maid, Liddy Smallbury, are sorting out papers and other relics of the lately dead owner when a horseman arrives and knocks at the door. Eventually Mrs Coggan, the cook, answers as Bathsheba is not presentable. It is Mr Boldwood, farmer of the adjoining land, come to pay his respects, and to ask about news of Fanny Robin. He is a rich forty-year-old bachelor, apparently immune to feminine charms, who had helped Fanny through school and to obtain a post in the house of Bathsheba's uncle.

Boldwood leaves, and the ladies talk, Bathsheba admitting that a man had once asked to marry her (she does not say that it was Gabriel Oak, now her shepherd!) but that she had refused him, as he was not good enough for her. They hear the farm-hands approaching.

early stage of Classic Renaissance This seventeen-century period in English architecture formed part of a general reversion to the classic principles of architecture, with fine planning, proportion and scale, coupled with a discriminating selection of ornament.

pilasters Rectangular columns, especially those built into a wall.

Gothic Architecturally the term indicates the pointed-arch style prevalent in Western Europe during the twelfth to sixteenth centuries. It includes the Early English, Decorated and Perpendicular styles.

houseleek or sengreen A plant with pink flowers growing on walls and roofs.

Terburg Usually Terborch (1617–81), a Dutch painter, considered the greatest of the Dutch 'little masters', painting life about him with impartial fidelity. He used colours sparingly, and glazed his canvases highly.

Gerard Douw A Dutch painter (1613–75), pupil of Rembrandt who developed minuteness and pseudo-realism of set pieces.

Normandy pippin A variety of apple.

thirtover Contrary, morose, unruly (dialect).

Little Weatherbury Or Lower Weatherbury; the name of the farm adjoining Upper Weatherbury (Boldwood's farm).

Avons and Derwents A fairly common name of English and Scottish rivers. The name 'Avon' is akin to 'afon' – river in Welsh, and to the Latin 'aqua' – water; and there are at least four notable Rivers Derwent in England.

pucker Dialect term for a state of perplexity, anxiety or confusion.

pelican in the wilderness See Psalm, cii,6.

Chain Salpae One of a group of marine animals, of many species. They are free swimming, and related to the lower vertebrates.

Russia duck A fine white linen canvas.

drabbet A drab twilled linen used for smock-frocks.

pattens Overshoes with a wooden sole on an iron ring for raising the wearer's shoes out of mud or water.

Philistines Biblically (see Judges, xvi,9) an ancient people living along the south-west coast of Palestine: they were alleged (we now know, quite erroneously) to be without artistic sensibility. Matthew Arnold used the term to denote narrow-minded uncultured people.

Chapter 10

Half an hour later Bathsheba tells the men of Bailiff Pennyways' dismissal, and informs them that from now on she is personally to run the estate. No news is yet known of Fanny Robin. Bathsheba speaks to each of her men, and some working-women, pays them their due, adding some extra as a present from her as the new farmer. Gabriel Oak is to have Cain Ball as his under-shepherd.

A man arrives from Casterbridge with the news that Fanny has gone off with the Eleventh Dragoon Guards, in which her young man is apparently a soldier, but not a private. Bathsheba arranges for Farmer Boldwood to be told. She clearly and coolly indicates that she is prepared to work hard for her farm, and that she expects her men to do so too.

Newmill Pond At Weatherbury.

Buck's Head See note p.20.

wimbling Twisting bands for the trussing of hay, faggots, etc.

Early Flourballs and Thompson's Wonderfuls Former varieties of potatoes, no longer cultivated.

gawkhammer Dialect term for an open-mouthed vacant fool.

hustings Platform from which (before 1812) Parliamentary candidates were nominated: hence often a scene of heckling and fierce political argument.

Abel The second son of Adam, slain by Cain, his elder brother. See Genesis, iv, 1–15.

Jove Popular name of Jupiter, the chief deity of Roman mythology, and identified with the Greek Zeus.

Olympus The highest peak (nearly 9600 feet) in the Greek peninsula, on the borders of Macedonia and Thessaly, and regarded as the home of the gods.

Eleventh Dragoon Guards Soldiers who took their name from the dragon, or short musket, which they carried: later they were essentially cavalry, until mechanized in the 1930s. The 11th never existed in fact.

Melchester Hardy's name for Salisbury, city and country town of

Wiltshire, standing on the Avon 84 miles (134 km) south-west of London. In glory is its fourteenth-century Early English cathedral: it has many fine and notable buildings, and is an agricultural and military centre.

'The Girl I Left Behind Me' An anonymous song and tune which can be traced back to the eighteenth century: it is traditionally associated with the British Army, being played on occasions of departure.

thesmothete A name given to certain judges and lawgivers of ancient Athens; hence, one who lays down the law.

Chapter 11

On a snowy evening in the dreary outskirts of a garrison town a young woman counts the windows along the barrack wall; upon reaching the fifth she attracts the attention of the occupant by throwing snowballs. A Sergeant Troy answers: Fanny Robin calls him her husband, yet asks him when they are to be married. In a halting conversation they arrange the calling of the banns of marriage in their respective parishes and a meeting the next day. As Fanny leaves, soldiers laugh within the barracks.

banns Notice is church of an intended marriage, read thrice over the preceding three weeks to allow opportunity of objection.

Mrs Twills's In Casterbridge (Dorchester), where Fanny has taken lodgings in following Troy.

Chapter 12

Next market-day at Casterbridge, at her first appearance as a farmer in the cornmarket, Bathsheba proves her many qualities, particularly as a good-looking woman; only one man ignores her completely. This is Farmer Boldwood. Liddy explains that there was some rumour of his having once been jilted, and this may be the cause of his deliberate aloofness.

Corn Exchange The central market for cereals: the following paragraphs of the text explain its methods of display and business. The present North Street building is not that of the novel's.

naïveté Artlessness, lack of affectation, innocent simplicity.

Roman features Aristocratic and dignified features, coupled with a proud, even arrogant bearing.

Chapter 13

One Sunday afternoon before St Valentine's Day Liddy and Bathsheba are conversing; the companion suggests that they use an old Bible and key to 'divine' or guess their future. Liddy talks of Boldwood at church that morning, who did not once turn his head to look at Bathsheba. Bathsheba is reminded of a valentine she has bought and, almost in jest, 'tossing' by means of a hymn-book – she decides to send it to Farmer Boldwood. The valentine bears a simple poem and is sealed with 'Marry Me'.

Sortes Sanctorum *Sortes* (Lat.) means a species of foretelling or
  divination performed by selecting passages from a book haphazardly:
  here it is from the Holy Bible. The method usually (though the details
  in the text are vague) is to open the book at random, and the passage
  you touch by chance with your finger (here it seems the key) is the
  'sacred' response. Here too, it seems that the selected verse is read out,
  and the person it brings to mind is to play a momentous part in
  Bathsheba's destiny.
post-octavo A size of paper, of indeterminable proportions, as the
  term is very unspecific.
Daniel The hero of the Biblical book of Daniel, who remained faithful
  to Jehovah through great trials and in spite of threats.

Chapter 14

Next evening Boldwood, in his comfortable bachelor home, surveys the letter, the valentine, gravely, as he has done ever since its arrival. What can it mean? Who has sent it? He rises with the dawn, and goes out to one of his fields, leaning on a gate as the mail-cart passes. He is handed a letter: however, it is not for him, but for Gabriel Oak. Seeing Oak's sturdy figure on the ridge going down to Warren's Malthouse, Boldwood follows.

Puritan Sunday The English Puritans of the sixteenth and succeeding
  centuries were strict Sabbatarians, and radically purified religion to a
  point of severe austerity and discipline.
Columbus It is recorded that as Christopher Columbus (1451–1506)
  on his fateful crossing to the New World in 1492 was about to give up
  and abandon his attempt, some floating seaweed was seen which gave
  him hope that land was near. It was, and the West Indies, and
  subsequently the Americas, were discovered.
ewe-lease A grass field or down stocked with sheep.
old Venetian glass Very fine glassware made in Venice in the sixteenth

century which, in technical and artistic perfection, had no equal in the world.

Revision questions on Chapters 9–14

1 Describe in your own words the exterior view of Bathsheba's house.

2 What are we told here about Farmer Boldwood?

3 Describe some of the farmwork detailed during Bathsheba's wage distribution. How does Bathsheba bear herself here?

4 What can we learn of Troy's character from his conversation with Fanny Robin?

5 Why, in your opinion, does Bathsheba send Boldwood the valentine?

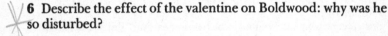

6 Describe the effect of the valentine on Boldwood: why was he so disturbed?

Chapter 15

In the tavern some farmhands are eating and talking, mainly about Bathsheba's inability to carry on alone and her 'fancy' feminine whims. Gabriel comes in with some new-born lambs, and amid other conversation he vigorously asserts that anyone who talks ill of Bathsheba will have to deal with him. The lambs revive; Gabriel feeds them, and then Boldwood enters, excusing himself for having opened Oak's letter which had been incorrectly addressed. Gabriel does not mind: it is from Fanny Robin, and he permits Boldwood to read its contents, which indicate that she is to be married to Sergeant Troy.

Boldwood knows something of the soldier's history and reputation, and is concerned. Oak has to leave hurriedly to attend to further lambing, and Boldwood hesitatingly follows, finally asking him if he recognizes the handwriting of the valentine. Oak, almost equally embarrassed, identifies it as Bathsheba's; the now tortured and restless Boldwood pretends to pass it off as a jest, but he returns home in acute mental discomfort.

hyperbolic curve A geometrical curve, formed by 'slicing' a cone so that the plane is at a greater angle to the base than that made by the side of the cone.

kerseymere Twilled fine woollen cloth.

Joey Iscariot Familiar name for Judas Iscariot, for whom see note, p.14.

entr'acte Strictly, the interval between two acts of a play, or a similar pause in which a dance or piece of music is performed.

harpsichord A keyboard instrument, resembling the grand piano, in which the strings were plucked or vibrated by quill or leather parts acted upon by depressing the keys.

tined Shut, closed (common in dialect).

Lady Day Name now applied to 25 March, the Feast of the Annunciation of the Virgin Mary; formerly also 8 December, the Conception of the Virgin; 8 September, the Nativity; and 15 August, the Assumption.

Sexajessamine As near as Joseph can get to Sexagesima, the second Sunday before Lent.

smack-and-coddle style Kiss-and-cuddle manner.

Thor The Scandinavian god of war and thunder: his hammer typified thunder and lightning, and had the virtue of coming back to him after it was thrown.

I'm a Dutchman A colloquial expression meaning, 'I'm not who I am in fact'; thus a verbal gesture of assertion.

Chapter 16

One morning at All Saints' Church in the barrack town the congregation is about to leave when a soldier, Sergeant Troy, marches in and is obviously waiting for his bride-to-be to arrive for the marriage ceremony. Half-an-hour passes: she does not arrive. The sergeant turns and leaves, soon to meet a flustered and frightened Fanny Robin in a nearby square. She has made a mistake, having gone and hopelessly waited at All Souls' church instead. She hopes they can marry tomorrow, but the sergeant walks briskly away without attempting to alleviate her obvious anxiety.

quarter-jack Mechanism to strike the quarters on a bell, often ending in a little figure of a man.

Chapter 17

Boldwood sees Bathsheba the following Saturday in Caster-bridge market-place: he looks at her closely, noting her beauty, which disturbs him profoundly. Bathsheba, still at a distance, knows she is being observed, and realizes that she has broken into the armour of Boldwood's aloofness. No word is exchanged between them, however.

R.A.'s Abbreviation for Royal Academicians, that is, those who have had their work admitted to the Royal Academy of Arts, the premier art-school and exhibition gallery of Great Britain.
'the injured lover's hell' The quotation is from Milton's *Paradise Lost* (Book V, lines 448–9): Nor jealousy/Was understood, the injur'd lover's hell.

Chapter 18

Farmer Boldwood is the most eminent man of the parish: a man of substance, and of strong feeling, serious and intense. His land adjoins that of Bathsheba, and soon after the distant encounter at Casterbridge, he sees her again in her fields, with Oak and his under-shepherd. He feels compelled to talk to her, and he walks over to where they are tending the lambs. Both Bathsheba and Oak look up as he nears, but he passes by in shyness and doubt. Bathsheba understands, intuitively, and resolves never again to disturb the even tenor of Boldwood's life.

roan and bay These are terms used to describe the colouring of horses: roan is reddish-brown, and bay more of a chestnut colour.
Moorish arch The typical Byzantine tall semicircular arch.
almonry A place where alms, or gifts to the poor, were distributed.
Dryads In classical mythology, tree-nymphs who lived in the trees and died when the tree died.
cabala Usually spelt cabbala. These were Jewish oral traditions, said to have been delivered to Moses by the priests and handed down through the generations only verbally: the term later included occult philosophy, and, by extension, is used to indicate some mystical, magical, puzzling and secret problem.

Chapter 19

Towards the end of May, Boldwood decides that he must talk to Bathsheba: he feels himself to be deeply in love, and that he has overcome his reticence. He seeks her where she is watching the sheep-washing. They converse: Boldwood soon makes an offer of marriage and a passionate declaration of his love. Bathsheba says that she cannot now answer, and must think carefully about the situation, but she does not leave him entirely without hope.

apotheosis Glorification or deification.

Cyclops' eye In Greek mythology the Cyclopes were giants with one
  eye in the middle of the forehead: in Homer's *Odyssey* they are
  represented as shepherds living in Sicily.

Revision questions on Chapters 15–19

1 Show how the relationship develops in these chapters between
Bathsheba and Boldwood.

2 What are the opinions of the 'rustics' concerning Gabriel Oak?

3 Give the gist of the conversations between Oak and Boldwood
concerning Fanny's letter and valentine.

4 What impressions are left of Troy and Fanny Robin from the
episode at the church?

5 Why did Boldwood not talk to Bathsheba at the scene of the
lamb-'taking', but only later at the sheep-washing?

Chapter 20

Bathsheba is not in love with Boldwood: the marriage would be
socially and financially commendable, but she cannot resolve her
doubts as to its wisdom. The next day she contrives to speak to
Gabriel Oak, alone, as he is grinding the shears for the sheep-
shearing. Oak, with his natural candour, expresses the view that
her conduct towards Boldwood is unworthy: Bathsheba is
furiously angry, and dismisses Gabriel from her farm. He leaves
at once.

Elizabeth in brain Queen Elizabeth I of England (reigned 1558–1603)
  had extraordinary political intelligence and a shrewd brain which
  outwitted every statesman in Europe.

Mary Stuart in spirit Mary Queen of Scots (1542–87), of legendary
  beauty, great courage and a passionate nature, was beheaded by
  Queen Elizabeth, who considered her a menace to her throne.

Eros In classical mythology the Greek name for Cupid, the god of love.

Ixion's punishment In Greek mythology a treacherous king who for
  boasting of having won the favours of Hera, was bound to a revolving
  wheel of fire in the Infernal regions.

Danby sunset The Danbys were a family of English painters. Francis

Danby (1793–1861) may be represented by his *Fisherman's Home-Sunset*, now in the National Gallery, London; his sons James Francis (1816–75) and Thomas (1817–86) were also well-known artists.
Moses The reference is vague, but the meaning clear: it could apply to Exodus, x,28–9.

Chapter 21

On the afternoon of the day after Gabriel's dismissal, a Sunday, Bathsheba's farmhands inform her excitedly that many of her sheep have broken through into a field of young clover which has bloated a number of them: some have already died. Only Gabriel Oak, locally, has the skill to operate on them sufficiently quickly for there to be any hope of saving the majority. Bathsheba is at first determined not to humble herself by sending for him: reluctantly she has to agree to do so, but Gabriel refuses to return unless he is asked for politely. This she does, pleadingly, and he returns with his instruments. He skilfully operates and saves all but a few of the stricken sheep. Bathsheba asks him to stay on, and he agrees.

blasted Blast is a flatulent disease of sheep.
Ephesians This New Testament book lies in between Corinthians and Thessalonians with Galatians on one side and Philippians and Colossians on the other: a little confusing!
Swoln with wind and the rank mist they drew A line from Milton's *Lycidas* (line 126).
vetches Tares: generally applied to cornfield weeds, though one species is grown as fodder.
Sixteen Acres ... Whitepits All these are names of fields.
lettre-de-cachet (Fr.). Originally a letter under the royal signet: usually a royal warrant for arrest and imprisonment.
trochar Usually trocar: a surgical instrument consisting of a perforator enclosed in a metal tube, and used for withdrawing fluid from a cavity; here it is for releasing air.
rumen The first stomach of a ruminant (cud-chewing) animal.

Chapter 22

On the first day of June the important task of shearing the sheep gets under way in the great shearing-barn: Bathsheba watches with concern and interest, and Oak shears away with an expert's speed and skill. Farmer Boldwood appears, and talks to Bathsheba; and Oak, rarely for him, snicks a sheep's skin.

Bathsheba goes off with Boldwood to look at his sheep, leaving Gabriel in charge; and the men conclude among themselves that this means a forthcoming marriage. Gabriel'sa thoughts are mixed, but he will permit no unpleasant rumours to be circulated.

moschatel A small herb with pale green flowers with a musky smell, found in shady places.

cuckoo-pint The wild Arum plant.

malachite A mineral of green colour, which can be highly polished.

ladies'-smocks Local name for the cuckoo-flower, a general term for various spring wild flowers.

toothwort A name given to two kinds of plant, but here the Lathraea is suggested; a leafless fleshy herb, parasitic on the roots of trees.

doleful-bells Dialect name given to some kind of plant, entirely unspecified in dialect dictionaries.

Hindoo Usually spelt Hindu: one who professes Hinduism, the majority religion of India. The social system consequent upon its religious tenets is aristocratic, with many castes or ranks in numerous grades, from the Brahmin down to the social 'outcast'.

for the nonce Expressly for a particular purpose.

chamfers Grooves or channels cut into the stone.

Guildenstern The quotation is uttered by the character of this name in Shakespeare's *Hamlet*, II,2,240.

dewlap Fold of loose skin which hangs down from the throat of cattle.

Aphrodite In classical mythology she was the Greek goddess of love, beauty and fertility: the name could derive from a Greek word for foam, and she is often pictured rising as if born from a foaming sea.

St John Long's death St John Long was a quack doctor (1798–1834) who became fashionable for his treatment of rheumatism and consumption by liniments and friction: he could not cure himself, however, and died of consumption.

mixen Dunghill. The proverbial saying means, 'Better marry a neighbour than a stranger from distant parts.'

spear-bed Patch of spear-grass.

rusty linsey Linsey is a mixture of linen and wool: the adjective here suggests both its colour and it rough-worn appearance.

Nicholas Poussin A great French classical painter (1594–1665).

snares and nets From Ecclesiastes, vii,26: 'And I find more bitter than death the woman whose heart is snares and nets.'

brandise Brandiron: a tripod stand for a kettle or a large pot.

biffins The biffin is a type of Norfolk cooking apple.

Chapter 23

The great shearing-supper now takes place: a more genial Farmer Boldwood displaces Gabriel at the bottom of the table; after an ample supper, the farmhands enjoy their songs. The evening fades into twilight: Boldwood talks to Bathsheba, and Gabriel plays his flute in accompaniment to her singing. When the others leave, Boldwood remains, Bathsheba eventually telling him to wait a few weeks more for her decision about marriage. This is enough for Boldwood, happy at the merest chance.

I've lost... not A country song, similar to the one below.

I sow'-ed th'e ... A country song attributed to a Mrs Fleetwood Habergham.

Silenus In Greek mythology the companion of Bacchus, a constant reveller, making music and drinking wine endlessly.

Chromis and Mnasylus In Virgil's *Eclogue* VI there are two young shepherds (perhaps satyrs or fauns) who find Silenus in a drunken sleep: they exact from him a song which he had promised them, and he begins to sing amid general delight.

Homer's heaven Homer's two epics the *Iliad* and the *Odyssey* (written probably about 1000BC) were classical national poems, creating almost a Greek religious system, now classified into a complicated mythology.

'The Banks of Allan Water' The words of this song are attributed to M. G. Lewis, and the air to which it is generally sung to C. E. Horn, who composed the tune to 'A Frog he would a-wooing go.'

attar Fragrance. The metaphor is from the name of a fragrant oil made from rose petals.

Keats John Keats (1795–1821): the first Romantic poet to be born, and the first do die, leaving behind a precious legacy of rich poetry. The particular reference here is to the first stanza of his *Ode to a Nightingale*.

Chapter 24

Later the same evening of the shearing-supper Bathsheba makes her nightly tour of the homestead: in the fir plantation her dress is caught up in the spur-wheel of a passing soldier, a dashing young sergeant who enjoys fully the experience of teasing Bathsheba while he tries to undo the twisted fabric. He is Sergeant Troy. Once released, Bathsheba runs home, where Liddy tells the discomfited girl something of Troy's history and reputation. Bathsheba, on reflection, is not sure that she has not in fact been a little too severe with him: after all, he did say that she was beautiful.

ninth plague of Egypt The falling of darkness. See Exodus, x,21–9.
genius loci The presiding deity or spirit of the place.
gimp Silk twist interlaced with wire or a coarse cord, once fashionable
(as here), for trimming wearing apparel.
Casterbridge Grammar School Dorchester Grammar School, Hardy's
own school. See section on 'The author and his work.'

Revision questions on Chapters 20–4

1 Why is Gabriel dismissed?

2 Describe the scene on the sheep pasture before and after
Oak's return. Why did he not come at Bathsheba's first message?

3 Give in your own words an impression of the sheep-shearing
scene and of the great barn in which it took place.

4 Why should Pennyways be at the shearing-supper?

5 Describe Troy's first encounter with Bathsheba. What does
she already know of him?

6 Is Chapter 24, in your opinion, a good point at which to
conclude a serial instalment? Give your reasons.

Chapter 25

Troy is described: he lives only for the day, honest with men and
dishonest with women, with few scruples but very winning ways.
His education is well above that of the average soldier, and he is
eloquent, especially in flattery: he can, however, be harsh. A
week or two after the incident in the fir plantation Troy appears
in Bathsheba's hayfield, helping with the hay harvest. As soon as
he sees the mistress he stops work and approaches her.

Cretan A degenerate liar.
Corinthian A licentious libertine (from the notorious licentiousness of
ancient Corinth).
passados Fencing term for the thrusts made with one foot advanced.

Chapter 26

Sergeant Troy expresses many gallantries and compliments to
an amused and partly flattered Bathsheba: he talks of her beauty

charmingly, and Bathsheba is fascinated by his adroit conversation. He gives her his watch: she is quite excited and flustered at his excessive praise, and wonders how much of it is really true.

penchant (Fr.) Inclination, taste, bias.

Terrible Ten The Ten Commandments.

Tophet A word allied in sense to the Hebrew 'Sheol' and the Greek 'Gehenna' and 'Hades'. It is applied to the Valley of Hinnom (2 Kings, xxiii,10) where idolatries were practised, and where later refuse and the bodies of animals and criminals were burned.

John Knox Scottish religious reformer (about 1515–72): a most vigorous zealot for the Protestant faith, he directed much of his inflexible purpose towards the correction of Mary Tudor (the 'gay young queen') in frequent addresses and fulminating sermons from the pulpit.

Qui aime bien châtie bien (Fr.) The English equivalent is 'Spare the rod and spoil the child.'

Earls of Severn The reputed family of Troy, on his father's side.

gin Snare.

Chapter 27

One day later Troy reappears just as Bathsheba is attempting to settle a swarm of bees in a hive. Troy volunteers his services, dons the necessary protective clothing and hives the bees. Bathsheba expresses a wish to see Troy's performance at the sword exercise, and the promises to meet him alone that same evening to witness this short display.

espalier Stakes or lattice-work on which fruit trees or ornamental shrubs are trained.

costard A kind of large apple.

quarrenden A variety of apple common in Somerset, Dorset and Devon.

Chapter 28

In an uncultivated patch in some ferns a mile away from her house Bathsheba, excited and a little nervous, meets Troy, ready with his sword. He performs various movements marvellously and expertly, cutting and thrusting, snipping off a stray lock of her hair and spiking a caterpillar on her dress, all with a razor-edge sword. Just before he leaves Troy picks up the lock of hair and pockets it. Bathsheba now feels powerless before him. He disappears, after having kissed her lips quickly; and Bathsheba is emotionally disturbed to the point of tears.

cuts, points and guards Sword movements.
broadsword A sword with a broad blade, and one or both edges sharpened, primarily designed for inflicting heavy cutting blows.
aurora militaris A warlike halo: compare the expression with *aurora borealis*, the northern lights.
Moses in Horeb Horeb is another name for Mount Sinai, near the eastern arm of the Red Sea, on which the law in the Old Testament was given by God to the patriarch Moses.

Chapter 29

Bathsheba is now in love with Troy, innocently and heedlessly; and Gabriel recognizes this headlong infatuation as potentially dangerous. He awaits an opportunity to talk to her about Boldwood's lingering courtship; but Bathsheba says that she must tell Farmer Boldwood that she has decided not to marry him. Oak also speaks of Sergeant Troy, whom he mistrusts: he begs her, out of the love he still feels for her, not to entangle herself with the soldier. Once more Bathsheba tells Oak to go: but out of loyalty, Oak will not again be dismissed out of hand. They part, and Gabriel sees Troy meet Bathsheba as night falls.

lymph Watery fluid which bathes all the tissues of the human body, conveying nutriment and helping to remove waste products.
Eros See note p.30.
'reck'd not her own rede' Ignored her own counsel: the adapted quotation is from Shakespeare's *Hamlet*, I,3,48: 'Himself the primrose paths of dalliance treads/And recks not his own rede.'
Hippocrates A Greek physician (born about 460 BC), known as the 'Father of Medicine': he was an acknowledged master of medicine in his lifetime, both as physician and surgeon, and his oath of service and the Hippocratic ethic established a standard of professional ideals still accepted. He wrote over sixty works: the particular reference here is to his *Aphorisms* 2, No. 46: 'When two pains occur together, but not in the same place, the more violent obscures the other.' It is indeed curious that Hardy should have known this rather obscure reference.

Revision questions on Chapters 25–9

1 Summarize the main features of Troy's character. Is he utterly false and wicked?

2 What different topics are covered in the long conversation between Bathsheba and Troy in Chapter 26? What effect has all this on Bathsheba?

3 Summarize the account of the hiving of the bees. Does this brief episode add anything to the story?

4 In what ways is the incident in the hollow amid the ferns a climax, in both the story and in the development of Bathsheba's feelings?

5 What is Oak's stated opinion of Troy?

6 How does Oak this time respond to Bathsheba's demand for his dismissal?

Chapter 30

Later that night Bathsheba, excited and flushed, enters her house. Troy has just left her, and has again kissed her: he has to go to Bath and be away for two days. Bathsheba writes her refusal of marriage to Boldwood, and wishing to have it delivered by one of her maids, hears them discussing her and Troy, whom she defends. She then reveals her feelings to Liddy, who promises not to say a word.

Bath A city of Somerset, 11 miles (18 km) east-south-east of Bristol, in the Avon valley. It has a long history as a health resort (the springs were known to the Romans) and it remains one of the most impressive cities in the United Kingdom, with a long history as a centre of fashion (as many of Jane Austen's heroines knew), fine historic buildings, and striking street architecture, much in local stone.

Union The parish workhouse, dating from 1697, as a culmination of Poor Law Acts going back to 1601, in which the poor were relieved by having work found for them, with their children put out as a apprentices (remember the origins of Dickens's *Oliver Twist*, among others). In 1834 a union of parishes replaced the single parish as the area, boards of governors superseding the overseers, the necessary finances being subsidized by the rates.

Amazonian Of the Amazons; in Greek legend, a race of fierce warrior women.

Chapter 31

The next day Bathsheba meets Boldwood, the one person she is obviously most anxious to avoid. His feelings remain unchanged, and he asks for pity: in a fury of emotion he accuses Troy of having come between them, and considers it crass folly on Bathsheba's part to be so utterly and quickly infatuated by the soldier. Bathsheba asserts herself in Troy's defence, and Boldwood fervently threatens to punish Troy physically when and if they should chance to meet. On Boldwood's departure, Bathsheba thinks deeply on what to do, and as night falls she thinks longingly of her absent soldier-lover.

Yalbury Unspecified area (with no exact geographical site) outside Casterbridge on the road to Weatherbury.
tergiversation Evasive fickle conduct.
Amaranthine Purple.

Chapter 32

Late at night the quiet of Weatherbury and of Bathsheba's house is disturbed by the noise of a horse and carriage on the road: a solitary servant (Liddy is away at her sister's), seeing whom she suspects to be a thief in the paddock, rouses Oak and Coggan. They identify the distant trot as that of Bathsheba's horse Daisy. Hurriedly they borrow two of Boldwood's horses and pursue the trail to the turnpike. There they encounter Bathsheba herself, who coolly explains that she is going away to Bath. The men decide to keep quiet about the whole adventure: Bathsheba is clearly going off to meet Troy, her lover.

Longpuddle Lane A road leading from Weatherbury to Sherborne.
pinchbeck repeater A repeater is a striking watch: pinchbeck is an alloy, named after its inventor, of copper and zinc.
Sherton Turnpike The turnpike gate on the Longpuddle Lane (see note above).

Chapter 33

A week passes before a note comes to Weatherbury saying that Bathsheba will probably return a week hence: the oat-harvest begins in hot dry weather. Cain Ball rushes to the fields one day with the news that he has seen Bathsheba and Troy walking along arm-in-arm in Bath: Coggan and Gabriel, each in his own way, accept the news resignedly.

Gilpin's rig 'Rig' here means frolic or spree, and the reference is to the hero of William Cowper's mock-ballad *The Diverting History of John Gilpin*, who has many adventures on horseback in an attempt to accompany his wife and family in a carriage.

Lammas Sky Lammas is the festival of the wheat harvest, observed in the English church on 1 August; here the term indicates the clear hot weather of late summer.

Pilgrim's Progress See note p.22.

Sermon on the Mount The name given to the collection of sayings of Christ comprising Matthew, v,3–12.

Tom Putt A kind of apple.

Rathe-ripe Also rathripe and rarepipe: an early fruiting apple.

stun-poll Dialect term for a stupid fellow: a blockhead, dolt or dunce.

batty-cake A small cake: why it should so be called continues to puzzle dialect specialists.

trendle Baker's trough for mixing dough.

White Tuesdays See note on 'White Monday', p.21.

Moses and Aaron These two Old Testament figures are usually represented artistically with full and flowing beards.

High Church Of a Church of England party which exalts the priesthood and the saving grace of sacraments.

High Chapel The strictest sect of a lesser or inferior place of worship than the Established Church.

Matthew See Matthew, xxi,42–4.

Shimel, the son of Gera See 2 Samuel, xvi,5–14 and xix,18–23.

Revision questions on Chapters 30–3

1 What are the servants saying about Troy? How does Bathsheba react to this?

2 Give the gist of Bathsheba's conversation with Boldwood on Yalbury Hill. What does Boldwood have to say about Troy?

3 How did Bathsheba plan to reach Bath? What changes in her plan did she have to make, and why?

4 What work is now being done in the fields?

5 What has Cain Ball to say about Bath, and how do the others react to all his news?

Chapter 34

Bathsheba and Liddy return home together: Oak is greatly relieved. Boldwood, who had remained within his home since his last encounter with Bathsheba, calls on her to beg forgiveness: he is not permitted to enter, and assumes he remains unforgiven. As he turns away he sees Troy: he insists on speaking to him. Boldwood tells Troy that he ought to marry Fanny Robin, and that he is prepared to settle money on her to that end; further, that Troy should leave Weatherbury and Bathsheba that very night. He hands over some money directly. Troy takes it, but says that he has to speak to Bathsheba, who then appears, telling Troy (with Boldwood unseen in the background) to come to her, alone, that night.

A now perplexed and fevered Boldwood makes a further gesture and proposition, that Troy should marry Bathsheba: he, Boldwood, will abandon her to her delusions, so long as Troy shows that he really loves her and will not desert or hurt her in any way: and he will give Troy money so that he can purchase a military discharge at once and settle down. They walk to Bathsheba's home: Troy enters, and reappears with a newspaper, showing Boldwood the announcement of his marriage to Bathsheba in a church in Bath. He mocks Boldwood's utter discomfiture, and throws his money into the road. To Troy's laughter Boldwood utters dire revenge. Boldwood spends the night walking about over the hills and fields.

sovereigns The sovereign, as a single coin, replaced the guinea in 1817: it has now been entirely replaced by banknotes.
surrogate's The deputy of a bishop for granting marriage licences.
St Ambrose's Church Bath.
Fort meeting Feeble Figurative way of saying 'Strength against Weakness': the phrase has a French flavour.
Shade ... Acheron Acheron was a river of Thesprotia in the southern Epirus. In its upper course it ran through several gloomy gorges, and it disappeared underground at several points. It was therefore reputed to lead to Hades, and an oracle of the dead was situated on it: and all around lingered the souls of the departed.

Chapter 35

Very early next morning, indeed before five o'clock, Gabriel and Coggan, moving towards the fields, see Troy at an upper window of Bathsheba's house: Coggan at once exclaims that she has married him, while Oak is silently appalled. Troy cheerfully greets them, and talks airily of redecorating the gloomy house, and tosses them a coin. Boldwood passes on horseback, his face drained of colour, a man filled with grief and agony.

Chapter 36

One night at the end of August, Gabriel Oak, seeing every sign of imminent storm and heavy rains, surveys with dismay eight unprotected ricks in Bathsheba's yard. This was to be the night of the harvest supper dance. Troy insists that it will not rain, and the revelry continues as combination of harvest home and wedding feast. Troy is himself drinking heavily and plying the men, far less accustomed to strong drink than he, with far too much, despite Bathsheba's unheeded (and indeed derided) protests. She and the women and children leave: Oak stays awhile, and then quietly moves off to his home.

On the way his expert eye notes every sign of an impending storm, and he reckons up the enormous financial loss Bathsheba will sustain. He is determined not to let this happen: he tries to find help, but in the barn everyone is now quite overcome and helpless with drink. He moves on to the village to obtain Laban Tall's key to the granary, and from there he drags out the large rick-cloths to cover the wheat: but the barley will have to be thatched over.

'The Soldier's Joy' This is recorded as a traditional country dance, and was well-known in 1809 in the north of England.

St Vitus's dance A popular name for chorea, a spasmodic affection of the nervous system characterized by irregular involuntary movements, among other disorders. The name comes from sufferers resorting to the shrine of St Vitus, who was reputed to have the power of cure.

DD From the text this must mean two octaves lower than 'middle D'.

show the white feather Indicate that they are cowards.

palimpsest A manuscript in which old writing has been rubbed out to make room for new.

thatching-beetle Heavy wooden mallet used for driving in stakes.

rick-stick A stick used in thatching.

spars Pointed U-shaped sticks used for fastening down the thatch.

staddles The platforms on which stacks or ricks are erected.

Chapter 37

Lightning and thunder crackle around Gabriel, high up on the stack as he begins his thatching: no rain has yet fallen, and the lightning plays about the metal tools. Gabriel sees Bathsheba in the yard: he tells her that her husband Troy is asleep in the barn, and ask her to help him by passing up the sheaves. The storm breaks violently, lightning striking Gabriel's ricking-rod and flashing down his improvised conductor along a tethering-chain to earth.

A tree on a nearby hill is struck: and the storm passes over. They look into the barn, seeing the still drunken men: and Bathsheba explains that she married Troy in a fit of jealousy and caprice, lest he should go off with another woman. Gabriel sees that she is tired; he works on alone, noting that a sudden change of wind signifies an imminent torrential downpour of rain.

majolica The name given to two kinds of ware, one an Italian enamelled ware covered with an opaque tin-enamel glaze; the other one covered with a semi-fluid paste of white or cream, on which designs were scratched. The bright starkness of sudden colour is here stressed.

Hinnom See note on 'Tophet', p.35.

Chapter 38

Three hours later dawn breaks, and Oak is still working away. The rain begins to fall and he is soon soaked through; at seven o'clock he is finished, and he sees the revellers sheepishly (all but Troy, of course) making their way home. He goes off too, and meets Boldwood. He learns that Boldwood's ricks too are uncovered and will be almost totally lost: they have been over-looked, and this for Boldwood, is a most telling confession. He reveals something of his bitterness and dire melancholy.

Flaxman's group John Flaxman (1755–1826) was a notable English sculptor: in 1775 he began to be regularly employed by the famous Wedgwood firm of potters to design classical figures and medallions for their chinaware. The reference here is to a classical sketch of this type now in the Royal Academy, London.

prepared a gourd See Jonah, iv, 6.

Revision questions on Chapters 34–8

1 Why did Bathsheba not admit Boldwood to her house on her return from Bath?

2 Why is the second part of Chapter 34 called 'A Trickster'? Why should Troy behave as he does?

3 What sums of money does Boldwood offer Troy, and for what purposes?

4 Comment on the differing reactions of Oak and Coggan on realizing that Troy is married to Bathsheba.

5 Describe 'The Revel'. Why are the farmworkers so ready to acquiesce in Troy's every proposal?

6 What natural signs does Oak read of the imminent storm?

Chapter 39

One Saturday evening in October Bathsheba and Troy are returning from market in their gig up Yalbury Hill: he is walking alongside, still soldierly and erect, and grumbling at his hard luck and bad losses at Budmouth races. He has, to Bathsheba's misery, lost over a £100 in a month; but her tears are scoffed at. She asks him to promise not to attend the second meeting: Troy retorts with derision.

On the brow of the hill they meet a poor-looking sad woman who asks about the Casterbridge workhouse: Troy starts at the voice; the woman sees and recognizes him, and swoons. Troy tells Bathsheba to continue her journey while he talks to the woman, who is, of course, the desperate Fanny Robin: she recovers a little. Troy gives her what money he has, and arranges to meet her on Monday to give her some more and to find her shelter. He rejoins Bathsheba in the gig, admitting to his wife that he knew the woman on the road but refusing to comment on the matter at any length.

Budmouth This is Hardy's name for Weymouth. It has been a popular holiday resort since the time of George III, and has had a long and interesting history.

Union-house See note on 'Union', p.37.

Grey's Bridge Stone bridge (usually 'Gray's Bridge') over the Cerne at Casterbridge.

Chapter 40

Poor feeble Fanny Robin struggles on towards Casterbridge; she sleeps a little under a haystack, awaking at night to see the distant lights of the town. Onward she labours, improvising a pair of crutches for support, falling and staggering on her way. Slowly, painfully, she crawls on: a friendly dog accompanies her on her way. Eventually she reaches the Union house, and falls prostrate at its threshold. Later, someone appears, and the pathetic figure is carried inside.

Jacquet Droz A Swiss mechanic and inventor of great ingenuity (1721–90).

Juggernaut A title of the Hindu god Vishnu, whose cult is celebrated by thousands of pilgrims, taking several days to drag the god's chariot through deep sand to his country house: tales exist (largely untrue) of pilgrims being crushed to death in vast numbers during the process, though accidents are frequent; and occasionally a fanatical pilgrim has thrown himself under the enormous wheels in the hope of immediate salvation.

Durnover Moor See note p.21.

Newfoundland, mastiff, bloodhound Three popular breeds of dog; the first large and strong; the mastiff a particularly powerful dog with a large head, drooping ears and pendulous lips; and the last a very keen-scented dog formerly used in tracking large game, stolen cattle or fugitives.

Pleiads See note on 'Pleiades', p.15.

Chapter 41

The next day after the incident on the road is Sunday: Troy asks Bathsheba for £20. He wants it for Fanny Robin; Bathsheba assumes it is for the second Budmouth race-meeting on Monday, and they bicker, although Bathsheba eventually takes the money from her housekeeping funds. She sees a slip of hair in Troy's watch: it is not hers, for it is yellow in colour: and Troy talks lightly of a young girl he had intended to marry before he had met Bathsheba, and goes on to say that it was from the woman they had met on Yalbury Hill. Bathsheba feels cruelly treated, and weeps when he leaves, repenting her folly and the loss of her independence and integrity.

Next day she learns that Troy has left the house early. Boldwood appears, talking to Gabriel: they then converse with

Joseph Poorgrass, who comes over to tell Bathsheba that Fanny Robin has died in the Casterbridge Union and that Boldwood (who has now gone) is arranging to have Joseph go to Casterbridge to bring home her body for the funeral. Bathsheba insists that she does this last service: she arranges the details with Poorgrass, who tells her some of Fanny's recent miserable history, some of which has already been strongly suspected by Bathsheba herself, much to her disturbance. Poorgrass goes off; Bathsheba learns now from Liddy that Fanny Robin's lover was a soldier, very like Sergeant Troy it was said, and that her hair was golden.

non lucendo Not shining, i.e. not clear (of an incredible explanation); inexplicable.

Diana The Artemis of the Greeks, Diana was the Roman goddess of hunting, nature, chastity, who also presided over childbirth.

use nor principal i.e. for interest (on the money or the capital). A term ignorantly applied from a different field.

neshness Dialect term for weakness or delicate health.

limber Spry, nimble.

laurustinus An evergreen shrub with oblong leaves, having large clusters of small white flowers and dark blue berries.

box A hardy native shrub, with a wood of close and fine grain.

boy's-love A staple in all village posies, the southern-wood plant *Artemisia abrotanum*.

Chapter 42

Joseph Poorgrass reaches the Union house: the coffin is loaded on to his wagon, someone chalking a few words on the top. Joseph takes the formal papers, arranges the plants and flowers, and sets off back to Weatherbury. An autumn fog comes up, enveloping everything, and the dispirited Poorgrass stops at the Buck's Head Inn, at Roy-Town, for a drink. Here he meets two of his friends, Jan Coggan and Mark Clark. The three gossip over their drink, and Joseph is prevailed upon – without much resistance – to sit longer and drink more, and several hours pass.

An angry Gabriel Oak appears, scolding Joseph for his untrustworthiness: and he goes off to drive away the hearse himself, reaching Bathsheba's house quite late. The parson tells him that the funeral will now have to take place the next morning: the coffin is taken into Bathsheba's house, and raised on two benches in a little room near the hall. Before he leaves Gabriel rubs off the words 'and child', leaving only the name 'Fanny Robin' scrawled on the coffin lid.

Traitor's Gate The gloomy passage by which traitors entered the Tower of London.
'Malbrook' The anglicized name of a French nursery ditty, 'Malbrouck, s'en va-t-en guerre', dating from the eighteenth century. The tune in Britain is to that of 'For he's a jolly good fellow' and 'We won't go home till morning': it has had great popularity all over Europe to many different sets of words.
grim Leveller i.e. Death. A poem by James Shirley (1596–1666) is often entitled *Death the Leveller*: it is to be found in most anthologies.
vis-à-vis Face-to-face.
To-mor-row, to-mor-row! Obviously from a local song.
King Noah The Biblical Noah as referred to by an ignorant man with a poor knowledge of the Bible.
Eleventh The Eleventh Dragoon Guards, Troy's old Regiment.' See note, p.24.

Revision questions on Chapters 39–42

1 Describe the encounter with Fanny on Yalbury Hill: why does she faint away?

2 Why is Fanny Robin's walk into Casterbridge so painful and distressing, both to her and to the reader?

3 Comment on the episode of the dog.

4 Show how the chance glimpse of the hair in Troy's watch has significant consequences.

5 What additional news is given of Fanny Robin's recent movements?

6 Why does Bathsheba question Joseph so closely on the details of Fanny's death?

7 Describe the scene at the Buck's Head.

Chapter 43

Later that same night a tearful Bathsheba, awaiting the arrival of Troy, is so wretched that she feels that she must talk to someone, preferably to Gabriel, who would tell her the truth. But her determination fails her on reaching his cottage. Bathsheba returns home, and finds her own proof by unscrewing the coffin lid. There lies the golden head of Fanny Robin with her baby: Bathsheba kneels and prays by the coffin. Suddenly Troy appears, takes in the scene, and then he sinks to his knees in remorse, kissing the dead woman's lips. Troy spurns the desperate, frantic Bathsheba, admitting his guilt, and telling Bathsheba that Fanny is his real wife: Bathsheba runs out of the house in anguish.

Esther to this poor Vashti Esther is the chief character of the Old Testament book bearing her name. When Vashti, the consort of the Persian king Ahasuerus was deposed, Esther, the adopted daughter of Mordecai, a Jewish exile, was chosen in her place.

Mosaic law A great deal of the Pentateuch, the first five books of the Bible (called the Books of Moses) is taken up with the severe laws and ordinances decreed for the Jewish people: the direct reference here is to Exodus xxi,23–5.

Tετέλεσται In Hardy the cap T is not in italics. This Greek word means 'It is finished'. See John xix,30.

Chapter 44

Bathsheba runs into a thicket and sleeps until dawn, when Liddy finds her. Fanny is to be buried at nine o'clock, and mistress and maid wander about until then, returning to a disused attic of the house. Bathsheba is resolved to hole herself away in the attic for a suitable time: she hears that a grand tombstone is to be erected on the site of Fanny Robin's grave.

'like ghosts from an enchanter fleeing' The quotation forms most of the third line of Shelley's 'Ode to the West Wind'.

collect A short prayer which precedes the reading of the epistle in the Mass of the Roman Catholic Church, and the Holy Communion Service of the Church of England. It varies with the day; the term itself is from the Late Latin 'collecta', meaning an assembly.

Beaumont and Fletcher's *Maid's Tragedy* Francis Beaumont (1584–1616) and John Fletcher (1579–1625) were poets and dramatists: this play appeared in 1619.

Mourning Bride A tragedy by Congreve, produced in 1697. The first line is famous – 'Music has charms to soothe a savage breast.'

Night Thoughts A poem of some 10,000 lines of blank verse, in nine books, by Edward Young, published 1742–5: it is part reflection of life's vicissitudes, part soliloquy, and culminates in 'The Consolation', a song of the wonders of the night sky.

Vanity of Human Wishes A poem by Samuel Johnson, published in 1749, an imitation of the Tenth Satire of Juvenal. It considers the various objects of human ambition, and indicates their overall vanity.

Love in a Village A comic opera in three acts, composed by T. A. Arne and others, and first produced at Covent Garden in 1762. The librettist was the dramatist Isaac Bickerstaffe.

Maid of the Mill Another successful three-act opera, the words again by Bickerstaffe, and the music by Samuel Arnold: this was first produced at Covent Garden in 1765.

Doctor Syntax Verses written by William Combe (1741–1823) to accompany Rowlandson's drawing of the adventures of 'Dr Syntax', a grotesque figure of a clergyman and schoolmaster, who sets out to 'make a Tour and Write It' and meets with a series of amusing misfortunes.

Spectator A periodical conducted by Richard Steele and Joseph Addison from 1 March 1711 until December 1712, and revived later by Addison in 1714, when eighty more numbers were issued. It succeeded *The Tatler* and appeared daily: its avowed object was 'to enliven morality with wit, and temper wit with morality'.

Prisoners' base Often found as 'prison-base' or 'prison-bars': a boys' game, chiefly in running and being pursued from goals or bases.

Chapter 45

We here go back to Troy's activities after Bathsheba's flight from the house. He had replaced the coffin lid, spent a wretched sleepless night, and with all the money he could muster, including £20 from Bathsheba, he ordered a tomb for Fanny Robin's grave. Much later that evening he plants flowers upon the new grave by lantern light. It begins to rain. His work unfinished, Troy gropes for the church porch, and there falls asleep.

crocketed Ornamented with curved and bent foliage.

picotees These are carnations with petals edged with a colour contrasting with the basic tint.

summer's farewell Local name for two plants, a variety of Michaelmas daisy and the ragwort: the former is suggested here.

meadow-saffron A tuberous-rooted perennial, also known as the autumn crocus: it has pale purple crocus-like flowers which appear in autumn; the long slender lance-shaped leaves appear in spring.

Chapter 46

The rain increases: Troy sleeps on. An overhanging gurgoyle of Weatherbury Church spouts a violent torrent of water directly into Fanny Robin's grave, filling it with mud and completely ruining Troy's plants. He awakes, remembers that he has to finish decorating the tombstone and sees the dreadful ravage of the rain.

Dejectedly, he bitterly reviews his fate; he leaves the village secretly and unobserved. Bathsheba, still self-imprisoned, comes down when she hears that Troy has gone (it is believed to Budmouth), and visits Fanny's tomb. Oak is there too, and both see Troy's tender inscription. Oak replaces the earth, and Bathsheba replants the flowers, and directs that the leadwork of the gurgoyle be redirected to prevent any recurrence of this mishap.

Gurgoyle Usually and more commonly 'gargoyle': this is a grotesquely ornamented spout projecting from a high church gutter to carry the rain clear of the walls.

Gothic art See note p.23.

griffin A fabulous animal having the head and wings of an eagle, and the body and hindquarters of a lion.

parabola One of the conic sections. It is the plane curve formed by the intersection of a cone at an angle parallel to the side of a cone. Compare note on 'hyperbolic curve', p.27.

Ruysdael Jacob van Ruysdael (about 1628–82), one of the most celebrated of the Dutch landscape artists. The prevailing colour in his work is a full rich green.

Hobbema Meyndert Hobbema (1638–1709), a Dutch painter friend and probably the pupil of Ruysdael: they often worked together on tours, even painting the same views. Hobbema's favourite landscape is that of a tree-studded and well-watered countryside.

'He that is accursed . . . still' The meaning is clear, but the quotation is apparently a paraphrase of Galatians, i,8–9.

Chapter 47

Full of remorse and gloom, Troy wanders off towards the coast: he wishes to bathe, and undresses, swimming out beyond some rocks. He is caught in a brisk current off Budmouth, and nearly drowned; by sheer luck he is rescued by the passing boat's crew of a brig: he is given some clothes and taken back to the ship.

Balboa's gaze The reference is to Vasco Nunez de Balboa (about 1475–1517) the Spanish explorer and conquistador who, in September 1513, was the first European to set eyes upon the Pacific Ocean, from the peaks of Darien on the Isthmus of Panama.

pillars of Hercules The ancient name for the rocks forming the entrance to the Mediterranean.

Gonzalo The honest old counsellor in Shakespeare's *Tempest*.
en papillon This presumably means 'butterfly stroke', but the term is not recorded as such in French dictionaries.

Revision questions on Chapters 43–7

1 What is, in fact, 'Fanny's Revenge'? On whom does the vengeance fall?

2 Describe Troy's reactions upon seeing the dead woman.

3 What is the purpose of the natural description in the early port of Chapter 44?

4 Why does Bathsheba decide to shut herself away?

5 Why does Troy decorate Fanny's grave as he does?

6 Describe the episode of the gurgoyle. Do you think this is merely grotesque, or is it also unbelievably coincidental? What are the reactions of Troy and Bathsheba to this startling event?

Chapter 48

Troy remains away for some time, much to Bathsheba's relief; but she feels he will again return, and that will mean the end of any reasonable future for her and her farm. She is at Caster-bridge when she hears a report that Troy has drowned: his clothes have been found, and no trace of his body: Boldwood catches her as she swoons at the news. She returns home, silent and thoughtful. A newspaper arrives containing an eyewitness account of Troy's drowning; later his clothes are sent to her. She looks at the coil of Fanny Robin's yellow hair, and decides to preserve it as a keepsake.

Lulwind Cove Lulworth Cove, near Weymouth. It is a circular bay about five hundred yards across and almost enclosed by hills. Some editions have 'Luistead'.

Chapter 49

Winter follows: Oak is made bailiff; Boldwood lives gloomily apart and alone, neglecting his farm; and he asks Oak to super-intend his Lower Farm. Bathsheba assents reluctantly: and Oak is now a happier man, paid by Bathsheba, and sharing Boldwood's profits; yet he still lives the simple life he has known before. Boldwood, some nine months after Troy's disappearance, tentatively re-opens his marriage proposals: he is prepared to wait, even for six years, for Bathsheba's hand.

dand Dandy (Dorset dialect).
Jacob Younger son of Isaac and Rebekah (Genesis, xxv) who served his uncle Laban for fourteen years as a shepherd and obtained first Leah and then Rachel as his wives.
Greenhill Fair See note on 'Greenhill', p.21.

Chapter 50

The annual autumn sheep fair at Greenhill is held, and both Bathsheba and Boldwood have large flocks there, attended by Oak and Cain Ball. There is also a circus, with an equestrian performance by none other than Troy. The story of his wanderings is told: now he is a circus performer, with Bathsheba in the audience. Troy sees her, and, in some confusion, tells his manager that he will perform his piece in dumb-show: and he carefully adds to his disguise before entering the ring.

At the evening performance he knows himself to have been recognized by Pennyways, Bathsheba's ex-bailiff: he hears him and Bathsheba talking, with the ex-bailiff handing her a note. Troy sees all this through a slit in the canvas: and from there he skilfully snatches the note held now in Bathsheba's fingers. The message told her that her husband was alive and present: Troy decides that he must quickly befriend Pennyways.

Nijni Novgorod The old name for the city of Russia now called Gorky. One of its suburbs (Kunavino) was the site from 1817 of the great annual fair (25 July – 10 September) at which the products of the country for hundreds of miles around were sold and exchanged.
Kingsbere Hardy's name for the village of Bere Regis, a few miles from Dorchester, on the skirts of Egdon Heath.
South Downs Usually Southdown: a short-woolled breed of sheep from the chalky soils of the Sussex Downs.
Oxfordshire A short-wool breed of sheep from this region of England.
Leicesters A long-wool breed, particularly found in East and North Yorkshire and Durham, and used extensively for cross-breeding.
Cotswolds An exceptionally hardy breed of the Gloucestershire hills, and one of the oldest-established.

Exmoors A horned breed of Devon moorland sheep, with a close fine fleece and rendering fine mutton.

Turpin's Ride Dick Turpin (1706–1739) was a notorious English horse-thief, whose story was particularly romanticized by Harrison Ainsworth's *Rookwood*: to avoid capture, he rode from London to York on his horse Black Bess. The story is pure fiction. Turpin met his fate on the scaffold.

Rembrandt effects The emphasis here is upon the effects of the light and the paintings of the great Dutch artist Rembrandt Harmensz van Rijn (1606–69) reveal a master's touch in his handling of light and shade, especially in interiors wherein strong light falls from outside.

Pennyways See the end of Chapter 8 of the text.

penetralia Innermost parts.

'Major Malley's Reel' This country dance is twice mentioned in Hardy's works.

Chapter 51

On the way back to Weatherbury, Boldwood accompanies Bathsheba, she in her gig, he as an outrider on horseback. He asks her directly about a possible marriage: she makes no promise, going only so far as to say that she will tell him her decision at Christmas. Weeks pass: she discusses her situation with Gabriel Oak, who offers sound and sensible advice, without any mention of his own love for her.

Chapter 52

Boldwood's Christmas party is held: Bathsheba knows that she is its principal cause, and is anxious; Boldwood, for him, is almost gay with expectation. But Troy, behind the scenes at Caster-bridge, is busy hatching his plans with Pennyways. He decides to confront the pair personally.

croquet-playing Croquet is a game in which wooden balls are driven by means of long-handled mallets through a series of hoops or arches: it is usually played on lawns in the summer.

Shadrach, Meschach, and Abednego The story is told in *Daniel* of these three Jews who refused to worship the golden image set up by Nebuchadnezzar. For this they were cast into a fiery furnace, but God preserved them.

The White Hart This tavern stands, at the eastern entrance to Casterbridge, close to the bridge.

ayless Always.

lammocken Clumsy, slouching (widespread in dialect).
scram Puny, withered (S.W. England dialect).
plimmed Swelled (provincial dialect).
pommy Pulped apples crushed for cider (S. England dialect).
strawmote Stalk of straw (S.W. England dialect).
scroff Rubbish, refuse (S.W. England dialect).
Juno A very important goddess of Roman mythology one of the great and powerful goddesses of the Roman State, closely associated with women.
Noachian cut As of the time of Noah; here old-fashioned and unconventional: Troy, of course, is using it in part-disguise.
Alonzo the Brave A ballad by M. G. Lewis (1775–1818).

Chapter 53

As the dancing and enjoyment continue Bathsheba decides to leave Boldwood's party, but the farmer appears, asking her the fateful question. Boldwood openly declares his love: he is still prepared to wait, and slips a ring on Bathsheba's finger. A stranger is announced, and in walks Troy, with a laugh, demanding his wife and pulling at her arm. Suddenly a shot rings out: Boldwood has snatched up a gun from the rack and in his fury has killed Troy. He very nearly succeeds in turning the gun next upon himself, a move prevented by his servant. He leaves, after kissing Bathsheba's hand.

Concurritur – Horae Momento The title may be thus translated, 'The battle is joined: all occurs within the short space of an hour.'
gutta serena Strictly a medical term, a symptom of which Hardy describes: it is a blindness without any outward change in the eye.

Chapter 54

Boldwood immediately surrenders himself to the law: Weatherbury is in a ferment. A cool Bathsheba has Troy's body taken away to her own house. By the time the doctor arrives Bathsheba has singlehandedly washed and laid out her dead husband. Then her strength gives out; Liddy, alone with her mistress, hears her spend the night in remorseful anguish.

the gaol Dorchester County Gaol, standing on the high ground over the Frome. In the meadows below people used to assemble to watch the hangings which took place on the level roofs over the gateway.

Melpomene The Muse of Tragedy, one of the nine Greek deities of poetry, literature, music and dance.

Chapter 55

The following March the trial of Boldwood takes place: evidence is gathered pointing to his mental instability. He was pathetically obsessed with the prospect of marriage to Bathsheba, to the extent of hoarding, in a locked room, expensive clothes and jewellery, all labelled with what would have been her married name, Bathsheba Boldwood. He pleads guilty and is sentenced to death, but a petition to the Home Secretary helps to commute the sentence to one of life imprisonment.

javelin-men A body of men in the retinue of a sheriff, carrying spears or pikes, and escorting the judges at their assizes.
Decalogue The Ten Commandments.
First dead . . . forth he yode From Sir Walter Scott's metrical romance 'Marmion' (1808).

Chapter 56

Spring comes: Bathsheba has withdrawn into herself. As the summer passes she moves about a little more, and one day enters the churchyard, tearfully surveying the double grave of Fanny and Troy. Oak is there, and tells her that he is thinking of leaving England for California. Bathsheba is troubled indeed: Oak seems deliberately to be keeping his distance. She calls on him, and he tells her that he is now not going to emigrate, but is arranging to take over Boldwood's farm and leave her service. He tells her of local gossip: and professes his love and his wish to marry her. A strong affection still blinds them after so many years of nearness and mutual understanding, far beyond and more lasting than mere fleeting passion.

Lead, kindly Light This and the next two quotations are lines from a hymn, written by J. H. Newman (1801–1890), in 1833.
Lady-day Now only 25 March, the Feast of the Annunciation; it was formerly also 8 December, the Conception of the Virgin; 8 September the Nativity; and 15 August, the Assumption.
W. Barnes Dorset poet (1801–86), a farmer's son, who took Holy Orders, and wrote a number of poems in the Dorset dialect, all pleasantly perceptive of rural charms.

Chapter 57

Oak and Bathsheba are to marry, by licence, within a day or so. It is to be a quiet and simple affair. Both arrange for the ceremony to be performed almost as a routine: a damp misty day helps to shroud their secret. Newly married, they return to Bathsheba's home for tea. Suddenly there is a tremendous noise: all the men are there with the Weatherbury band, in celebration. The farmhands rejoice, and the talkative Joseph Poorgrass has the last word on the matter, prompted especially by Oak's speaking of 'my wife' as if they had been married for twenty years.

Went up the hill side . . . bride Hardy's novels contain many references to country ditties popular in his day.

As though a rose should shut and be a bud again A beautiful line from Keats' 'Eve of St Agnes', Stanza 27.

serpent An obsolete bass wind instrument of deep tone, about eight feet long, made of wood covered with leather and formed into three U-shaped turns.

hautboy The earlier name for the oboe, a double-reed woodwind instrument of treble pitch, from the French 'haut bois' – a tall length of wood.

tenor-viol The viola, a four-stringed instrument, slightly larger than a violin.

Marlborough John Churchill, 1st Duke of Marlborough (1650–1722): an English soldier who commanded the British and Dutch Forces in a series of brilliant campaigns, and was victorious over the French at Blenheim (1704), Ramillies (1706), Oudenarde (1708) and Malplaquet (1709).

'Ephraim . . . alone' The quotation occurs in Hosea, iv,17.

Revision questions on Chapters 48–57

1 These ten chapters formed the last instalment of the original serial. Do you think that they could be split into two sections? Give your reasons for dividing them up, or retaining them as they stand.

2 Detail the information provided which suggests that Troy had been drowned.

3 Describe the events at the Greenhill Sheep Fair.

4 What are the feelings of Boldwood, Bathsheba and Troy as the hour of the Christmas Eve party draws near?

5 Why did Boldwood not kill himself?

6 What evidence was produced at Boldwood's trial to suggest that he was mentally unbalanced?

7 In your opinion, is the commuted sentence of life imprisonment a fair one?

8 Oak does not actually propose to Bathsheba. On what understanding then do they marry?

The characters

Certain factors must be grasped before one can estimate fairly Hardy's considerable achievement in characterization. Firstly, this novel was conceived and planned as a monthly serial and thus the characters are introduced gradually, one after the other as a rule, until their personalities, characters and inter-relationships are firmly established in the reader's mind as the story runs its course. This can of course, be a method of present-ation in other kinds of novel: but the serial shape usually demands this piecemeal introduction, with dominant characters and characteristics firmly established in sequence: often we hear about someone well before he is physically introduced, and our expectation of his full and personal entry is already coloured and conditioned by what we have heard (e.g. Troy, in 8: Boldwood in 9). Secondly, one must appreciate Hardy's tragic, not necessarily entirely pessimistic, view of life, much more fully and powerfully projected in his later novels. He believed (as did every good Victorian) that 'The wages of sin is death'; and, less conventionally that mankind was prone to disappointment and pain, strife and melancholy in the huge impersonal mechanism of a relentless Nature.

Thus Hardy's characters are subject to what they may believe to be chance and coincidence, just as much as Hardy himself believed in them: but there are vast forces ranged against them from which there is no evasion. They are to be seen as puppets manipulated by a grand scheme beyond their will. There is no struggling clear from one's past: one must reap the whirlwind; and this is obviously true for all the major characters excepting Oak, and even he pays the price for his outright honesty and integrity. Coupled with this, too, runs a cynical, sceptical view of human happiness, especially of that conventionally linked with religion, love and marriage. The blind 'Immanent Will' renders much of human activity negative and ironical, yet through his characters in their dilemmas Hardy reveals, without bitterness, his selfless pity, sympathy and charity for his tormented suf-ferers.

Next one must note Hardy's fondness for revealing character

traits directly from his point of view, instead of his shaping situations within the plot to expose these traits by what his characters actually say and do. Many pages are studded with Hardy's own exposed analyses of his characters (e.g. the first six paragraphs of Chapter 1, much of 12, almost all of 18, the first seven paragraphs of 29). This can be obtrusive, and it is sometimes overdone, but it tends to a swifter pace, economy and clearer direction. The characters are quickly made positive and real, and their strongest characteristics are clearly and simply revealed and emphasized. There are no mysteries, hardly any subtleties, no puzzles or intellectual intricacies to solve, no elaboration or sophistication to cut through in what, after all, Hardy himself modestly called 'these imperfect little dramas of country life and passion'. Yet we must also note, as he says (not of himself, in fact, but so by inference) in *The Woodlanders* that he grew up in

one of those sequestered spots outside the gates of the world where may usually be found more meditation than action, and more listlessness than meditation; where reasoning proceeds on narrower premises, and results in inferences wildly imaginative; yet where, from time to time, dramas of a grandeur and unity truly Sophoclean are enacted in the real, by virtue of the concentrated passions and closely-knit interdependence of the lives therein.

This charges his characters with their power and force, sometimes even with grandeur, and gives them a stature of universal significance based on elemental, everyday and commonplace issues.

It should be further noted, but not overstressed (and some qualifications will be added under the individual character sketches which follow) that Hardy arranges his characters often rather mechanically, in positions of balance and counterpoise. Oak counterbalances Troy, with Boldwood necessarily hopelessly cast in between. Fanny Robin also is a counterweight to Troy, revealing aspects of his nature before he enters the stronger love-triangle; she also represents what Bathsheba could have been, and perhaps would have been, but for the turns and twists of fate. There are other 'balances' between mistress and maid, mistress and shepherd, Troy and Boldwood, and so on, which are 'tipped' at different times, according to situation, all stressing in the eventual direction Hardy wishes his story to tend. Thus, in the long view, Hardy is less a novelist of character than of situation, though his characters, nevertheless (as already indicated and later to be detailed) are alive, forceful and credible.

Finally it must be seen that the plot (and therefore its players) is dominated by the passions of men and women in love; in short, by sexual longing and possession. For we see here some of the torment and agony caused by and for love: how some are sacrificed and humiliated because of it, others purified and elevated; how there is true and false love, neither easily nor readily recognized; how it can ennoble, degrade, and kindle worthy or ignoble passions. This factor helps to make the plot and characters akin to those of the old ballads of English literature, so dearly loved and so sharply remembered by Hardy from his boyhood and youth: Bathsheba seems to reign in a court with her retainers, amid intrigue and ardour; and these imaginative creations are often invested with a kind of poetic quality of timelessness and grandeur, with a fundamental significance for all who wish to understand.

Bathsheba Everdene

A headstrong maid, that's what she is

Bathsheba dominates the novel, from her splendid entry in Chapter 1 to our last sight of her, smiling and at last contentedly married at the end of Chapter 57. She is fascinating because she is a complex character, unlike all the others, and unlike them too in that she develops and changes markedly as the novel progresses.

The earlier part of the book stresses her high-spirited vanity and provocative capriciousness. Her spirit is decided and independent, and she is practical when she so chooses. We see all this in her entry into Oak's village and her disdain for his help (1), her prompt decision to ride side-saddle (2) and her actual tomboyish performance on horseback (3). It is emphasized by her touches of materialism: Bathsheba will not be taken for granted in a 'man's world'. Vain she may be: but she is a 'new woman', striving for independence and emancipation, especially from men beneath her in education and assurance. She is also self-confessedly 'too wild', wishing always to win, and yet demanding to be tamed by a stronger personality. She in fact exhibits, in this phase, a 'Jekyll and Hyde' complexity that is probably in all of us, certainly in our youth (she is little more than twenty), only she is frank about these irrational and masterful urges in her young mind. Here Bathsheba is just a country girl, with all the freshness and practical nature that one instantly associates with such, fundamentally good-hearted even in her vanity and teasing, a girlish rebel, yet determined not to fall too soon into the conventional routine of the married women of her class and locality.

This 'dual' personality is again to be noted in what may be called the second phase, up to the intrusion of Troy into her life. It must be remembered here that Bathsheba herself is also an intruder in many ways: by origin (on which the old maltster and others comment tartly in Chapter 8); by her better education, and, of course, by her own, old, wilful desire for independence. Fate has decreed that she has to take over her dead uncle's farm, and she does so with a sure grip, and is resolved to do well and set a superior example in doing it. She is clearly businesslike and capable, showing abundant good sense and foresight in her farm management. Bathsheba shows much of her great courage too in her first public appearance at the Casterbridge cornmarket as the only woman farmer there: she uses no feminine wiles to her advantage: the farmers shrewdly believe her to be headstrong, but they accept her, and deal with her. Her self-reliance appears successful.

However, the other side, a negative side, also appears. Her vanity persists in that she regards the aloof and inattentive Boldwood as a black sheep, and this vanity leads to her feminine perversity and well-nigh freakish behaviour in sending Boldwood the valentine. This crucial fateful gesture takes us into the passionate heart of the story. Having sported with Oak's genuine affections, and now in a superior position by fate, she playfully, however innocently, disturbs the delicate equilibrium of Boldwood's emotions. The whole of his shame, agony and tragedy spring from this capricious action. Bathsheba is still, at this stage, full of the 'Old Eve': but her present position, and her destiny, will not allow such behaviour to pass unregarded. Boldwood's discreet pursuit of her affections reveals her greatest vulnerability: she is out of her depth when confronted with emotional conflict. Oak's swift courtship, though serious for him, she had treated playfully: he is almost ridiculed. Boldwood's emotion (not necessarily his love) is obviously stronger and more powerful: and Bathsheba proves her rapid growth in sense and maturity when she resolves never again to do anything which will disturb the settled pattern of his ways. However, this comes too late for both of them.

Bathsheba's emotional immaturity, her vanity and her fickleness have brought her to a crucial brink, and she falls an easy victim to a soldier's flattery, blandishments and glitter. It is all part of feminine folly, and she must share some of the blame with her tinsel-lover. Truth be told, Bathsheba is something of a flirt; but with Troy she burns her fingers. She knows he is flattering her, her unconventional rebellious nature seems to mirror his, and, of course, he woos and wins her much less woodenly than Oak and much less broodingly and obsessively than Boldwood. Troy wins her because he has played on the conventional frailties of woman-kind, and because he seems to want her as a woman, not as a mere possession. Bathsheba discovers her error soon enough after marriage: just as Boldwood's pent-up and frustrated affections pour out as a consequence of Bathsheba's intrusion, so her own long-suppressed feelings and passion are released by Troy's heartless, but blissful intervention: quite shamelessly she pursues him to Bath, and in a fit of jealousy, longing and distraction, marries him.

The marriage is a misalliance from the start: the realization of this enormously deepens and widens her character. For the rest of the novel, up almost to the last page, all Bathsheba's reserves of courage and willpower are demanded. She becomes more sympathetic to others, knowing the depths of pain from her own experience; she is more open to advice; she gains enormous strength from her afflictions, not least because she realizes that she is herself partly to blame. Her earlier resourcefulness, endurance and courage are indeed needed in the dark progress of a bitter marriage with a cruel and spendthrift husband, with certain knowledge of his liaison with a poor country-lass, once one of her own servants, through his alleged death and taunting return, culminating in his murder, with his killer, the man she had almost been prepared to accept in remarriage, condemned to lifelong imprisonment.

Bathsheba faces life squarely amid all this distress (and is the first of Hardy's heroines so to do): and she attracts our sympathy, despite her frailties and often petulant intentions. Her greatest weakness was in loving Troy, which she does sincerely. This he does not deserve: but there it is. It is all part of fate. She is sacrificed on the altar of this misplaced love, and only the steadfastness of Oak can restore something of her balance. But not all. Hardy's view of a happy marriage (end of 56) may be cynical: but, in this situation it is concrete. The passion has been spent: a true love remains. She can no longer laugh readily: she has matured prodigiously in three years or so, retaining her charm and regaining her buoyancy, after having been whipped by fate into a deeper comprehension of the dangers of independence in a man's world – in any world – and of the ironies and realities of existence generally: and she is still only twenty-three or twenty-four years of age at the end of the story.

Some other, minor but contributory, pointers to her character should be briefly mentioned. Note her love of nature and wild life, her interest in music and books, her capable adaptation of tone and manner towards different people in varying circumstances, and her physical appearance, admired by many.

Hardy comments, at a most dramatic and poignant moment of the story (54,377) that Bathsheba 'was of the stuff of which great men's mothers are made'; she is indeed cast in a heroic mould. We can see how she represents and typifies two sides of the currency of life, the wrongs done by women to men, and the greater and more crushing wrongs done by men to women. Bathsheba is the central figure who affects the lives of every other character in the story, and all are poor human puppets bandied about by fate. But unlike most of Hardy's heroines, and despite all her frailties, she is at least no hostage to fate, and is 'rescued' throughout the novel, and finally, by the quiet tenacity and shockproof integrity of her first lover, Gabriel Oak. It says much for her, perhaps everything, that at the last she realizes his true worth.

Gabriel Oak

Generous and true

Oak persists: he is there at the beginning and at the end of the story, and is the presence, active or passive, in all but twenty-two of the fifty-seven chapters, and is mentioned too in some of these. He is idealized in that it is difficult, almost impossible indeed, to find some human fault or frailty in him: but some there are, and these very weaknesses reflect a greater strength. To some extent he is wooden, in his stolid unbending endurance: but this is part of his nature as a child of the soil in the traditional agricultural life he typifies, and even symbolizes. Gabriel Oak does develop from an almost comic portrayal at the beginning (1,1–3) into the sober faithful persistent hero whose advice is sought and taken by his 'superiors' in station. He may perhaps be considered best under three broad aspects: as a farmer and shepherd, as a lover, and as a personification of integrity; of course he is often these simultaneously, and there are other traits of his personality shown.

The bachelor of twenty-eight, at the beginning of the story, has much to be proud of. His figure is youthful and lithe, his physique is imposing; he is industrious, and has been a good son; he has an unsentimental tenderness towards his animal charges: all these mark a countryman of 'quiet energy' and moral fibre. Gabriel Oak has a natural dignity and strength: and he is not unaware of the natural beauty which surrounds him. But he is the complete shepherd and farmer: his library may be small but it is not merely practical, and his efficiency is marked in every aspect of the agricultural seasonal round.

The unfolding chapters detail the farming year, and Oak's deliberate figure is seen at the lambing, making a lamb 'take' (18), sheep-washing, grinding shears, performing surgery on the blasted sheep, shearing (at the rate of nearly three an hour), scything the harvest, thatching (in the worst possible, and even highly dangerous, conditions), superintending two general farms of 2000 acres in all, and moving valuable sheep to exhibition. Oak progresses from a bankrupt ruined by cruel mischance to a bailiff and proprietor, all by his own tenacity and efforts. He can tell the hour by the stars (his watch, unlike Troy's, is unserviceable); he can track a horse, and know when it is becoming lame; he can eat, drink and sleep 'rough' as well as any man if he has to; and, moreover, he can charm away the time, and entertain himself by playing his flute: he also plays it well enough to entice a few coins from some hiring fair stragglers, to earn praise from a critical audience and to accompany Bathsheba – in a most ironic song (23). It is almost superfluous to point out Oak's resourcefulness in quelling the fire, operating on the sheep, thatching the ricks and so on: he is thoroughly efficient, dependable and imperturbable.

As a lover Oak is less successful: but then the term has 'romantic' overtones which Gabriel would scorn to acknowledge. He is attracted to Bathsheba and his fundamentally simple and unsophisticated nature, his origins and class do not make his proposal silly or Bathsheba's flighty rebuff any less hurtful. He offers all he has, and promises nothing he is not sure of providing. Neither the aloof dignity of Boldwood nor the trumpery glitter of the redcoat – both selfishly in love – can match Gabriel's unselfish, disinterested and sincere love. He declares that he will love, long for, and keep wanting Bathsheba until he dies: and he means it and does so.

Gabriel Oak waits through the thick and thin of Fate's worst pressures, never forcing his attentions, never flattering, always speaking his mind yet recognizing intuitively when to remain silent, protecting Bathsheba in every way he can from the inevitable consequences of her impulsive whims, which he watches so pitifully. He wins, at long last, not through the passion or burning ardour which cannot last, but by proving his moral integrity, his steadfastness, his patience and resilience. In the long run he must win in the competition of the rich possessive Boldwood and the materialistic Troy: their ardour is more of an outward show, the one as a result of overlong suppression and frustration, the other as a means to an end. The concluding passage of Chapter 56; 'Theirs was that substantial affection . . . evanescent as steam' may not be everyone's formula for a happy marriage, but few will doubt that it is a substantial foundation for mutual respect and a long partnership.

Oak's personal integrity is obviously part and parcel of his occupational efficiency and of his patient love of the woman who first rebuffed and humiliated him: but throughout the book his probity, restraint and self-mastery are emphasized. He never loses his natural dignity: his stoical resignation in the face of trouble is amazing. Bathsheba ridicules him; he loses his livelihood; he is superseded by two men. One, Boldwood, to whom he defers as befits the rich farmer's conventional status, he understands: the other, Troy, he openly disapproves of and disbelieves, and is humiliated by him. However, Gabriel waits: indestructible, solid, even for some chapters rather wooden, and his star shines at the last.

Clear glimpses are given of other attractive aspects of his nature. He is no fervent churchgoer, but he prays on his knees at night. He is homely and natural, yet proud of his efficiency, and never afraid to express his innermost feelings, more out of his essential simplicity than any premeditation. He is generous, financially, out of a lean pocket to Fanny Robin, but always and throughout to Bathsheba in his energy and time and good advice; though he will not be taken for granted. Gabriel never disparages Boldwood, which is indeed magnanimous. His tender-hearted humanity emerges in countless situations: note especially his thoughts on the disastrous loss of his sheep (5), and his removal of the telling chalk mark on Fanny's coffin (42), and throughout his treatment of his animals, be they sheep, dogs or horses.

Oak counterbalances all the other major characters by his fidelity and staunchness to those principles of decent life, belief and social living which Hardy thought valuable, part of the unique legacy of the agricultural tradition in a country's character and soundness. He is perhaps too unaggressive: here he seems to share Hardy's own lack of ambition. However, it is not by asserting oneself aggressively that one prospers, in the long run, but by patience, endurance, even humility. His emotions are not superficial; yet he is not led astray by them, and he does not yield to them.

In the physical and moral turmoil of the great storm, he alone rises above it by the purposeful tenacity with which he conquers it. And even Oak, because of this very unaggressiveness and lack of flattery, causes unhappiness to Bathsheba, who would often have wished his approval when he withholds it and who confuses his meekness with weakness when he is asked for a forthright opinion which then displeases her.

The sturdy enduring sheep-farmer, who moves from his smock frock at a hiring fair to his own cob, shining boots and a tall hat, and to the woman he loved from the first – his rivals so tragically removed – is aptly named. Master of himself, servile to none, Oak typifies and almost symbolizes an honest integrity, a rugged endurance, which we would like to possess, but fall far short through our pettiness and weaknesses. He may well be idealized: but the ideal he represents is an uncommonly fine goal for most of humanity.

Sergeant Frank Troy

He was a man to whom memories were an incumbrance, and anticipations a superfluity

Troy is an active, rarely passive, figure and must not be rapidly dismissed. It is too easy to condemn him quickly and completely as the typical Victorian villain of the piece, as if he were some obvious 'bounder' in a melodrama of the day. He happens to be selfish (no rare characteristic), opportunist and handsome: he is also a soldier, with the soldier's classic adaptability, swagger, pride in himself. Troy is reputed to be irresponsible where women and their affections are concerned. We shall of course consider his dark and ugly side: there is much of it. But we shall miss a great deal if we do not realize that even Troy has saving graces which Hardy clearly indicates, and we must not view him on too narrow or prejudiced grounds.

All regular soldiers on the march are intruders, especially so in the countryside of the period. They would seem to enjoy a freedom of movement, a breadth of travel, quite remarkable and even attractive to the stable inward-looking village communities along their route. We hear of them first quite early beating up for recruits in Casterbridge before leaving the town: the unemployed Oak almost wishes he had joined up. Next, with our hindsight of having read the novel, we realize that Fanny Robin, throbbing with love, excitement and expectation, is stealing away from security to follow her lover Troy, and the regiment is bound for Melchester and beyond.

Troy himself has not yet appeared: and even in Chapter 11, in which poor Fanny Robin talks with him from the other side of the barrack wall, we do not see him, but only hear his rather curt replies, once he has recovered from his surprise. But the last paragraph (96) is important and easily missed: Troy has been talking to Fanny, clearly his 'wife' (94) in fact but not in name, in the company of his comrades. As Fanny pathetically leaves, he utters some comment which provokes laughter: this leaves an unpleasant taste in one's mind. There is something rough and coarse here. His replies seem sincere enough: but on examination it is quite clear that he had hoped that Fanny had been just another girl 'at every port' to be readily abandoned and forgotten: a plaything to be trifled with. Here and elsewhere Troy reminds one of Bryon's cynical yet long-attested comment:

Man's love is of man's life a thing apart;
'Tis woman's whole existence.

Fanny has followed him, for love and security, which he had clearly promised: he has also promised to marry her, too, but he has of course made no preparations whatever to do so. Her pathetically hopeful letter to Oak and Boldwood's pertinent comments thereon (15,117)] are immensely ominous. The paragraph 'H'm – I'm afraid not ... silly girl!' deserves nothing: at last we have some concrete details of Troy's background, and there is no reason to doubt their general authenticity.

Troy keeps his word with Fanny about the wedding, however, (Chapter 16) and here he shows much courage, courtesy, restraint and resolution. It is an uncomfortable and embarrassing situation, and he manages it with considerable dignity and self-possession. The rather distracted and silly girl has made a foolish error: the worse that it has hurt Troy's pride. He is indifferent and callous on seeing her in all her fluster and weakness.

It is notable, and usefully coincidental, that over four months pass before Troy enters the main theme of the story, winter having passed into early summer, and that he returns to Weatherbury for his few weeks of leave, and not to or with Fanny Robin, who has clearly been abandoned to her fate, and put out of his mind. The explicit and revealing Chapter 25 gives us a full picture of Troy's mentality: his selfishness, his insincerity, his cynical attitude towards women; his irresponsibility and his opportunism are all made quite clear. The chapter is detailed, and must be re-read closely as a sourcebook for one side, the stronger side, of his personality.

Troy's whirlwind courtship of Bathsheba (remember that he marries her in July, having met her only the month before) is fascinating and masterly. It is no use, critically, to say that Bathsheba should *not* have become infatuated with one who seems to us to be an obvious scoundrel, an impudent flatterer, a smart dashing swashbuckler, an obvious breaker of hearts with a veneer of glamour. Much of this is hindsight in having read the novel, and a great deal of it is already known to Bathsheba anyway. It is what she chooses to believe that counts. She believes him when he tells her the tale of his origins, but Boldwood knows this much more accurately: she believes his story about his regular church-going, which Gabriel disproves at a glance. But love is blind, and Troy is no amateur lover.

The miraculous description of his sword-play (Chapter 28) must also be seen symbolically: it is also a physical attack, for Bathsheba's heart and womanhood are pierced. One must not overstress the fact (yet many Victorian eyebrows would have been raised at its obviousness) that Troy introduces powerful sexual symbols here and elsewhere: and later works of Hardy which we now read with perfect ease and equanimity indeed shocked many of his contemporary readers and reviewers. It is to misread, or to read the text carelessly, not to see the implications of Troy's brilliant sword-play (culminating in that so-distressing kiss), his inordinate delay in unravelling her dress from his spur, and his extraordinary and embarrassing haste in reaching the foot of the ladder on which Bathsheba is trying to hive the bees (27,185).

Troy is a strong masculine force, a virile figure of a man to the unworldly Fannys and Bathshebas encountered during his military movements about the world and countryside: his smart dress, his erect carriage, his dexterity, his above average intelligence and language all unite to make him a figure of conventional romance, ballad and legend. He has a hypnotic effect, certainly: but Bathsheba is no fool, and the strongest advice given her by both Oak and Boldwood warning her (quite selflessly as it happens) against him melts in the warmth of his ardour. Blind love wins, or blind fate: perhaps they are identical here. She pursues him, shamelessly, and from this marriage Troy develops as the author of Bathsheba's misfortunes.

It is not that he changes in character necessarily: his changed situation simply allows fuller scope for what we have known and suspected. Troy has married a beautiful and rich wife, which gives him a smug superiority over his rivals (the Boldwood – Troy encounter of 34,231–8 is indeed bitter and callous): it has permitted and paid for his easy release from the army to a life of leisure and pleasure. Earlier he has spent part of his leave helping with the hay-making: now he can afford to spend his time and his wife's money gambling at Budmouth races. Impulsive romance and impetuous passion have had their due effects: their continuation is now unnecessary and even tedious, and he chooses to continue the life of irresponsibility he had previously enjoyed in the army, without the army's cramping limitation of

personal freedom. The love Bathsheba has for him –
or for worse – has at last tamed her, and freed him to
becomes something of a rake's progress.

Now every worst aspect of Troy's personality is exposed: his
desire to change radically the very style and atmosphere of the
ancient and lovely house; his arrogance; his drunkenness; his
wilful assertion of his new-found authority – some ex-soldiers
never leave the army; his improvident gambling with his wife's
livelihood; his contempt for his wife's feelings in countless
incidents; and of course, his wilful misunderstanding or complete ignorance of the people and atmosphere into which he has
moved. One intruder has joined with another to disrupt and
disturb the long-established pattern of village life, and the consequences are stark and dramatic.

Yet the other side of Troy's nature is clearly revealed by the
chance encounter with Fanny Robin. He promises to help her
(unnecessarily abusive to his wife incidentally) as if his conscience pricks him, and he does tell Bathsheba much of the truth
later on. The money he borrows is not for gambling, but to help
Fanny. Again she does not appear, a smarting reminiscence of
the embarrassing marriage ceremony which never took place:
but he gambles only a little at the races, returning to the fearful
scene of Fanny, with his child, in the opened coffin in his house.
No one can here doubt the sincerity of Troy's remorse: few,
however could forgive his rejection of his legal wife. His quick
pride has been mortally wounded: he has been stripped of all his
glamour and glitter. His selfish love of Bathsheba cannot compare, now, with the tender weak surrender of the always helpless
and lovelorn maidservant.

All Troy's flamboyant romanticism of providing and then
decorating Fanny's grave is a poignant, almost macabre touch,
which ironic nature cannot accept as sufficient reckoning for his
wrongs done. The gurgoyle does its work, all is ruined and
rendered futile and irrevocable, and Troy miserably skulks away
in self-banishment and self-effacement. Everything and every-
body he has touched has been hurt or destroyed: and this does
not alter by his chance return after a series of interesting, but
unglamorous, adventures. Troy has come down to being a tour-
ing circus-turn: a long step indeed from the red-coated gallant
who brandished the miraculous sword in the hollow amid the
ferns. He becomes conspiratorial: he then unmasks himself to

wife callously after that most ironic welcome
...n too happy, Boldwood, and is shot dead by
...d.

...antic for whom Hardy allows some sympathy
...is then finally, and necessarily, withdrawn. His
...heba is selfish: it is a means to the end of his army
...d a life of boundless leisure which he has not the
chara... ...or skill to use properly, but only for the self-
satisfaction of having scored off his wife's earlier suitors. He
becomes at times contemptible. His better nature glitters in little
flashes, especially with regard to Fanny Robin; but he grows
callous in his indolence.

The externally imposed discipline of his long army career has
ill-fitted him for the responsibilities of normal 'civilian' life and
manners in the small close community into which he has thrust
himself. Victorians too would perhaps have seen some 'taint' of
aristocratic blood emerging in the latter stages of the story.
However, in his better moments, Troy is at least light-hearted
and dangerously masculine: he is warm-blooded and cheerful,
dashing and gaily fickle. His sins come home to roost: the relentless universe cannot recognize his futile repentance for the
shames he has committed by the strength of his desires. There is
something satisfying about Troy's terrible death: but a light,
surely, goes out in the world at that fearful moment.

Farmer William Boldwood

His equilibrium disturbed, he was in extremity at once

Boldwood can hardly be thought of apart from Troy, the
human author of his greatest (and Bathsheba's) misfortunes,
and against that red-coated heart-breaker he seems a very dull,
wooden, stiff man and lover. He is, however, interestingly and
intensely drawn, and enters the story by degrees. We hear first
his authoritative tap and deep voice enquiring about Fanny
Robin, and Liddy adds details as to his bachelor state, his dignity
and wealth. But above all his first 'hearsay' impression is one of
kindness, as shown in his care of Fanny Robin and his apparent
invulnerability to feminine charms and wiles.

This makes Boldwood Bathsheba's 'black sheep' at her début
at Casterbridge cornmarket, and there his strong features and

quiet dignity are fully described, prompting further information from Liddy, and the sending of that fateful valentine. The fact that it is so disturbing to Boldwood is surely intended to seem odd and curious: he is rich, he lives well, he is respected, and bachelorhood is no moral failing. But the true explanation comes, very fully, in Chapter 18. This is a very rare example in Hardy of almost an entire chapter being devoted to a drawing of a personality, and it is highly significant and explicit. The seeds are here being sown for much that will later become painful, even terrible.

Boldwood is not quite normal in his mind, but 'a hotbed of tropic intensity'. He is emotionally unstable, and all the pent-up repressions of his forty years are liable to explode at a touch. If the 'Old Eve' stirred in the capricious Bathsheba to make her send the valentine, it certainly stirs the 'Old Adam' in Boldwood to have received it, and to find that the sender was his neighbour-farmer, of undoubted charm and beauty, saying 'Marry Me'. That he cannot believe it a jest may seem odd, but this is explained by the cast of his mind and the total lack of humour he exhibits. Serious, he expects the rest of the world to take at least some things seriously, and this apparent invitation to marriage is surely, to him, no matter for foolish jests. Dire results follow in its wake for all the principal characters of the story.

He becomes obsessed with the notion of possessing Bathsheba: and by degrees, Bathsheba being at first unsure of *herself* emotionally, and then through Troy's audacious intervention, Boldwood represents a selfish love in its most fatal form. The serious, dignified, straightforward man becomes a slave to an overmastering passion in which there are, at times, touches of madness and bursts of lurking physical violence.

A further hint of possible madness comes in Troy's light words and Coggan's reply (35,241): and then, at the last, when all his hopes are irrevocably dashed by a laughing mocking Troy, Boldwood kills his rival. He is just prevented from turning the gun upon himself, and surrenders himself voluntarily to the law: only then do we realize something of the markedly neurotic stamp of the man. Boldwood must be noted as the most striking figure in the history of the novel – perhaps in all writing – of a man tortured by the furious desire to possess a woman, and the consequences of that desire.

It is depressing, and even horrifying, to realize how delicate is the path between sanity and insanity, one emotional surge being enough to thrust Boldwood towards his terrible end; it is particularly so when we consider other aspects of Boldwood's character before he is wrung on the rack of Bathsheba's whims and then emotionally plundered by Troy's calculated intervention. He is shy, obviously kind and wholehearted, handsome and dignified, quiet and reserved, observant and sensitive to natural beauty, respected by all, intelligent, and markedly polite.

Boldwood never trifles: Oak, whom he would inevitably supplant, supports his claim to Bathsheba; Boldwood, face to face with Troy, speaks openly, and begs the soldier never to abandon her. But 'No mother existed to absorb his devotion, no sister for his tenderness, no idle ties for sense' (18,128). The fiery intensity of his repressed ardour hurls this lonely man inevitably to sordid ruin. His integrity is shattered by his heart's distress, and he is resigned to bitter death: in a most moving passage he reveals a strength in his weakness, and a misery of the soul (38,259–61). Fate plays on him cruelly, indeed with him. Troy is apparently dead. Once more his desire seems to be reaching fruition, all that he ever said about the soldier now obviously true and verified in fact. Hope again germinates: he is prepared to wait six years, and even enjoy the waiting as a kind of blissful penance, knowing the inevitable ecstasy that would eventually be his.

Knowing even that Bathsheba cannot return his love Boldwood prepares for her assent on his Christmas party, despite forebodings and agony. The six-year courtship begins: 'I am happy now', and within a page it ends. Troy has reappeared, with a mocking laugh and a callous wrench of his wife's arm: Bathsheba's scream is followed by the shot that kills Troy, and the other that he had destined for himself. It is a man's reaction to an animal of prey, and a more humane law of this century recognizes the crime of passion as no premeditated murder. But Boldwood's surrender is expected of him: if he cannot die by his own hand, then he must by another's. He has given up all hope of happiness in life (like the earlier remorseful Troy, and not for such very different reasons). Yet the revelations of his trial are unexpectedly shocking to the senses.

Boldwood's moodiness was natural: but the derangement exposed is severe and pathetic. One paragraph alone (55,381) 'that he had been . . . in advance in every instance', shows he has moved from being highly neurotic to become what is called psychotic, that is abnormally mentally affected. The hoarded clothes, the labels, the dates, all bear witness to a profound psychological disturbance, usually termed a fetishism, in that these secretly bought and concealed clothes and jewellery are regarded irrationally with reverence and affection: and there are sexual overtones too to 'these pathetic evidences of a mind crazed with care and love'.

And at the end: has he not pleaded guilty, wishing to have done with life and its cruelties? He is sentenced to death. Fate still can twist the knife in the wound. The death sentence is commuted: and what more bitter final wrench can there be for a man of Boldwood's temperament, rooted in brooding passivity, with so much of the past to remember that he would rather but cannot forget, than lifelong imprisonment behind bars? Jan Coggan's joyous outburst (55,384) 'God's above the devil yet!' is sincere enough – for him – but the underlying irony and cynicism speaks volumes for Hardy's view of one's life and destiny, and for the terrible and irreparable wrongs done, even unwittingly, by women to men.

Fanny Robin

Poor little Fanny Robin

Fanny Robin, slight figure in herself, presents an interesting character in the structure of the story. Bathsheba and Troy move into Weatherbury as 'outsiders' while she; part of the local scene, thinks she is escaping from the village into a securer world by following Troy on his marches: both she and Bathsheba pursue the same man, and both are ruined by him. At the very moment of Oak's happy chance of meeting Bathsheba again through his resourcefulness in dealing with the fire, crowned with the success of gaining worthwhile employment, he is the sole witness of the fleeing maidservant, already described in vague, wistful, sad phrases, on her way out of Weatherbury, to which she will never again return alive.

Fanny Robin is linked instantly with Troy, has been helped kindly by Boldwood, and has been the youngest maid in Bathsheba's newly taken over household. Her frail body hides an intense and unselfish devotion to the philanderer Troy, and thus her career inseparably binds her to all the struggles and emotions of the major characters. The shadow of her destiny hangs over all the tragic elements of the story: Fanny's secret departure prompts Boldwood's first call at Bathsheba's house, with its consequences; with her Troy's cynical attitude towards women becomes practised and concretely evident; her death is tragic. Even in her coffin she is surrounded by macabre and poignant events: and in her very grave nature cannot let her soul rest in peace.

She is attended throughout by pathos: her throbbing excitement, her recent dejection, her conversation with Troy, her fluster and fatal error in mistaking the church of her marriage – all these form a pathetic, wretched background to the developing emotions and love scenes of the major characters, but proceeding in what seems a different space and time. We lose sight of her for a while, but she remains an inescapable anxiety to the reader, especially as a still unmarried Troy bursts into Weatherbury in full amorous flight.

Then of course, Fanny is involved in some of the most unforgettable scenes of the whole novel. In Chapter 39, by which stage the marriage of her soldier-lover and ex-mistress is already turning sour, the sad poverty-stricken figure of Fanny is seen trudging its way towards her sole remaining hope, the Casterbridge workhouse; and the chance encounter with Troy is poignant, with profound consequences to him and · his wondering wife.

Chapter 40, her last journey alive, is surely one of the most moving, not least in its restraint. She has been utterly abandoned: her painfully counted steps falter to utter helplessness and hopelessness; and then the understanding dog arrives, and supports her. No human aid appears, and the dog's intuitive and instinctive behaviour helps her in her hour of desperate need, an ironic comment on 'man's inhumanity to man'. She achieves her goal, but only just, and there dies in childbirth. Troy's child dies with her. Even here the irony is given a further twist. The harmless dog is stoned away. It may be mentioned that a deputation of six American humanitarians called on Hardy to protest at this cruel treatment of the dog: they utterly missed the point. There could hardly have been a more eloquent appeal for human kindness to animals, and further, equally explicit and implicit, for human kindness to humans themselves.

Fanny is dead: but the slight girl and her baby in the coffin exert a strong and at times macabre pressure on the remainder of the story. She is more effective and influential when dead, in some ways, than when alive. She forces a major climax in the separation of Troy and Bathsheba, and the grotesque coincidence of the gurgoyle's spouting a torrential downpour right into her grave, spoiling Troy's belated tenderness, is a stark reminder of nature's quirks, against which human caprice and romanticism seem puny and futile.

One cannot pretend to sound any depths in Fanny's character and personality: her destiny is to have none, and thus she becomes a pathetic example of the selfless, weak, willing spoils of a man's harsh world, of a man's animal nature. Yet it says much for Troy that, at heart, when he is not deceiving himself and is stripped of all his glamour, when he is faced with cruel reality of what he alone has done, he professes a sincere love for her unashamedly. It is one of the few moral actions for which he deserves credit: Fanny perhaps deserved a less selfish lover and a more congenial fate.

Lydia (Liddy) Smallbury

Like a little brook, though shallow, was always rippling

Bathsheba's personal maid is the youngest daughter of Billy Smallbury, and thus the granddaughter of Jacob and the great-granddaughter of the ancient maltster. She can be separated from the rest of the villagers owning to her comparatively elevated position among them by occupation and consequent privileges: and, as a close – the closest – companion to Bathsheba until her marriage and then in Bathsheba's estrangement and widowhood, she is seen and used as a confidante, as a sounding-board for Bathsheba's private opinions and soul-searchings. Liddy is one to whom Bathsheba can always turn in the man's world she has deliberately invaded.

She is interestingly described (9,81) as a typical English country-girl, of open-air colouring and plump features: one who is dutiful, not servile, retaining her local aptitude for gossip (natural enough in any villager) and often pleasantly ungrammatical in her speech. She is a mine of information, often of the spiced and romanticized kind, about the neighbourhood. Woman to woman, Liddy's talk is often about marriage and husbands: she first tells Bathsheba of Boldwood's kind nature, and of his shyness and aloof dignity where women are concerned.

Although Liddy often imagines herself as a lesser version of her mistress, bathing in her reflected glory, especially where Bathsheba is asserting her feminine independence, she retains a homely frankness, more of her simplicity than any calculation, although she is prepared to waver a little in her opinions to please her mistress. Liddy, however, is frank in facing up to Bathsheba about Troy: and, indeed, asks to be dismissed rather than bear with Bathsheba's love-inspired moods of dark fury. Bathsheba softens, and Liddy (of Bathsheba's age) agrees to remain: but she clearly tells her of her furious rages, and does not attempt to 'whiten' Troy's reputation in compensation. She acquiesces, not intending to leave Bathsheba companionless: but she does not reverse her opinions.

It is Liddy, of course, in her simple village superstition, who incites Bathsheba to that fateful move of the Sortes Sanctorum; and it is she who says of Boldwood that 'He'd worry to death', a shrewd premonition. But of course, Bathsheba is the stronger woman, and one must acknowledge that she is mostly to blame for the dire consequences of her action.

Liddy's visit to her married sister provides a useful moment for Bathsheba's pursuit of Troy (31) and for Bathsheba's slightly deceitful scheme of return: in the strongly emotional scenes which follow Liddy remains in the background. Once again her local knowledge of fact and rumour, this time of Fanny Robin and her yellow hair, is used to highlight an episode, and again more significantly in Chapter 43 where Fanny's child is hinted at. Then Liddy contributes to a symbolic touch, mentioned in the section on 'Sympathetic background', rescuing her fugitive mistress (44), by walking perilously over the swamp, and the two contrive the entertainment of the self-imposed imprisonment of Bathsheba. Note that Liddy is solicitous, that her suggestions are comforting if somewhat antiquated, and that she has been peeping, quite intelligently, into some of Bathsheba's inherited books.

For the remainder of the story Liddy stays very much in the background of events, naturally enough. She remains sensible and practical, and she is there at the revelation of Bathsheba's marriage to Oak and at the church is one of the very few at the actual ceremony. Dependable, slightly imitative, practical and pleasant, Liddy helps to reveal much of Bathsheba's feminine nature unknown and unknowable to the men eager to possess her: in her talkativeness, superstition, local familiarity and good spirits she is a true daughter of the village.

The local community

The Philistines

Far from the Madding Crowd ranks very high among the pastoral novels of English literature, and is perhaps the finest of them all. One of the major elements of this excellence is the description, characterization and conversation of the farm workers. These enter the story, usually in different groupings, throughout. They are there, part and parcel of the fabric of the story, part of the landscape as the labourers of the fields, providing a background, an atmosphere, which is unmistakably rich, earthy, and often comic.

Not in or of the 'plot', they are an essential thread running through it, occurring almost as a ballad chorus. Their conversation has some correspondence to stage dialogue in its direction, strength, and give-and-take of thrust. Fifteen or so are named, and most are individually characterized: some are colourless enough to be dismissed, as is Laban Tall, just as Susan Tall's husband (though there is more of him than this in fact), while others have a considerable part in their passive but alert watchfulness of the goings-on all around them, such as Jan Coggan and Joseph Poorgrass.

There is thus a strong limelight on this group in the novel, and many of the individuals are distinctively characterized quite early on. The notion of having the sleeping Gabriel Oak carried into Weatherbury by Billy Smallbury and Joseph Poorgrass is one of the few happy chances of the book: it is of course a technical device to remove us from one scene to another, and to remind us of Bathsheba's vanity, but it introduces us to the men of the village and their shrewd, tart views. Then we have that number of men making up a 'great company', all confused by the fire: but their talkativeness, mass ineffectiveness, brisk willingness to do something they know not what or how, is strongly indicated: and to them the fire is a great event, long to be chewed over.

It is in Chapter 8 that we first have a full introduction to the diversity in community of the labourers. The malthouse is their natural focus, then as now: here they can drink and gossip, with their oracles and orators enthroned. This is a splendid chapter, a bran-tub or 'lucky-dip' from which one can extract at random essential elements of Wessex life and lore. We note first the initial caution, properly due to one new in the village, and then the expansion of welcome once recognition is complete with the old maltster's long memory of Oak's grandparents. Outward physical features are detailed throughout, and characters revealed swiftly. This whole piece sets the pattern for their other interpolations.

They enjoy a long talk: they relish their ale, especially when it is 'on the house' by having been sent down from their superiors; and in the combination of beer and gossip they find ease and high content; not even the gritty bacon spoils the hour, but adds relish so long as one chews carefully. Their speech gives a strong impression of dialect, but is not in fact much removed from standard English: there is a biblical ring about its phrasing and cadence, and religious affairs and views are a staple item unto themselves.

There is a whimsical vein of comedy; above all in their pride in some small attainment, quite outside their own control, such as age, a tendency to blush, distinctive spelling, physique, and so on. They love sheer gossip: they preserve traditional memories of a better past, and have serious views on the changing present. They provide a mixed fund of authentic information and village tittle-tattle: but one is sure that they live hard and work hard, with a great capacity for enjoyment when they can snatch some leisure in good talk, reasonable beer, and music.

In later episodes other detail is given of their work (Chapters 10 and 22 in particular), and individuals begin to stand out, especially Coggan and Poorgrass; and we also see their behaviour at and reactions to the great festivals of the farming year: importantly, the shearing-supper (23), the harvest-supper and dance (36), and the entertainment of the Greenhill Sheep Fair (50). Of far greater importance, however, than any singling out of characters (and Hardy here demonstrates considerable powers of characterization within a limited stratum of society) is the recognition of certain fundamental aspects of their day-to-day lives and thoughts. They have no illusions about their rather hard lives: there is an air of acceptance and resignation underneath, and perhaps promoting, their moments of joyful talk and gossip.

Their work is hard, their hours long, they have no great talent in general (Oak, of course, is self-educated above this level) to enable them to rise above a humble station. Thus they are rather a primitive group socially, often with a lack of sentiment, reverence, and even kindliness; although only one of them, Pennyways, can be said to be calculatingly malicious. The Buck's Head episode (Chapter 42) is worth attention, for herein, from Joseph Poorgrass and his cronies, we have gathered up and crystallized many of the less pleasant aspects of their nature: it is not deliberate unpleasantness, but essentially a part of their earthy natural environment. They drink here to excess, and know it: Coggan's comments on the dead girl are true, even platitudes, but callous and unfeeling; churchgoers, they have little reverence but a clearly trouble-free conscience over doctrine, which makes for a rather complacent attitude towards religion, and some cynicism.

They are simple folk essentially: garrulous, with an antique simplicity: but certainly not the 'yokels' of joke, comedy or ignorance. They are shrewd, often whimsical, down-to-earth, with a distinct style of living and thinking, and a rich fund of anecdote and biblical reminiscence which gives all their words and works the colour of the past, in a pastoral and historic setting.

At this point it is pertinent to ask: are they real? Are they purely literary, or did such people ever exist? Critics have long taken directly opposite views. On the one hand: '...unmistakably brittle, decorative, fictitious, literary ...' on the other: 'Read a page of rustic talk in Mr Hardy, and you will think of Shakespeare: listen to an hour of rustic talk in Wessex, and you will think of Mr Hardy.' Are they speaking what could have been their own thoughts, or is it all Hardy's, being merely the mouthpiece, so to speak, of the author's own ideas? Certainly many of these local folk are clever, articulate, rarely suffering physical hardships natural to their actual condition; and they indulge in much eating, drinking and fun in a sort of idyllic existence.

We know from the records of the time that this was a period of economic distress. The food of many labourers was scanty, and even bad (like the 'blue-mouldy' cakes Cain Ball bought in Bath – and he ate them: 33,226); we know too that their clothing and shelter were poor (like that of many in Warren's malthouse), that old age brought real wretchedness and little more than the prospect of the Union workhouse, and that there were shockingly bad standards of health and sanitation. All this is indisputable fact: but it happens not to be the kind of fact around which Hardy chose to write his novel. The point is indeed a central, cardinal feature of Hardy's whole purpose and aim in his writing, and his treatment of the local community in this novel reveals his fundamental standpoint towards realism in atmosphere and characterization.

Hardy, in fact, selects carefully. Hints of all the hardships and shortcomings of rural life are to be found in the novel: but there is a deliberate restraint in emphasizing them. Hardy knew well both the primitive, even animal, nature of the peasant (much of it due to his environment), and his economic suffering. From his familiarity with and close observation of the country folk around him he also knew that certain qualities existed: a love of fun, good talk, plays of wit, sharp but friendly repartee, an ironic slant on life, and even, at times, an intuitive appreciation of the countryside atmosphere, and of music. Hardy chose rather to focus on such virtues – while not at all neglecting certain failings of sentiment and tenderness – rather than on the actual social discomfort of the period. The centre of his novel, here and in many others, is concerned with human love and passion: the pastoral scene is a setting, a background, but not its intellectual essence.

This selection of material, in fact, sharpens the vividness of Hardy's picture of the agricultural community. As he says in Chapter 2,26, 'In making even horizontal and clear inspections we colour and mould according to the wants within us whatever our eyes bring in.' That is, again in his own words, 'All art is approximate – not exact.' What Hardy wanted to extract from his observation and knowledge, and convey to the reader, was the essential core of human dignity exemplified by the labouring class under all its burdens.

Hardy's aim was to choose and extract the essential nature of his characters, and these selected details with his emphasis make for their vividness. Thus the characters are not necessarily typical of any rural community at any time: but they are derived from the behaviour, manners and conditions of the contemporary peasantry. The selection may be arbitrary; it may seem idealized at times: but no one can deny that the 'rustic chorus' has reality and force, and springs alive from the pages of the story. This reality is not that of a mere photograph. It has been made, derived from actual life by what Hardy himself called the necessity of disproportion: 'Art is a disproportioning (i.e. distorting, throwing out of proportion) of realities, to show more clearly the features that matter in those realities, which, if merely copied or reported inventorially, might possibly be observed, but would more probably to overlooked.' This view applies to all Hardy's work; it is a key to all his thought: 'This reproduction is achieved by seeing into the *heart of a thing*.'

Setting and plot

Setting

Although the heart of Hardy's Wessex lies in the county of Dorset, more particularly in the region of East Dorset surrounding Dorchester (Hardy's Casterbridge), 'The Hardy Country' of the Wessex Novels, of which *Far from the Madding Crowd* was the first, in fact extends from the Bristol Channel on the west to Windsor (Castle Royal) on the east, and from Oxford (Christminster) in the north to Portland Bill (The Beal) and Launceston (St Launce's) in the south and south-west respectively.

Historically Wessex, the kingdom of the West Saxons, covered the country between the Thames valley and the south coast, excepting the kingdoms of Kent and Sussex, and from AD 560 had some distinctive history among the warring tribes of the period. In 829 the King of Wessex (Egbert) was recognized as overlord of the other English kings; by Alfred the Great's death in 900 the King of Wessex was *de facto* lord of the rest of England. By the time of his son this vague sovereignty was translated into a definite mastery; thence Wessex became merely a geographical expression, without consequence until Hardy's fictional and nostalgic recreation as a background setting for most of his novels and beginning with his *Cornhill* serial of *Far from the Madding Crowd*. Hardy, in fact, in each of the Wessex novels, is recreating or re-animating an intensely local, limited, ageless atmosphere, often of a period before his birth or of his very early years: and this sensitive, detailed, vivid breathing of life into a rural setting is a deliberate and essential factor in his thought.

For Hardy believed that there was something noble and disciplined, even grand, in man's association with the soil; that the rural community had an integrity and a self-sufficiency which urban life had lost or was losing; that intrusion of this urban life into the stable rural scene disturbed, temporarily and even tragically, the even tenor of agricultural life until it was eventually modified, adapted, and 'conditioned' to suit the small community.

Hardy knew, and this is even more important, that agriculture was decaying with improvements in railroad communications and in the more attractive urban amenities. Old values, based on the land and its folk, were being set at naught: rural integrity and simplicity were dissolving: a collapse of a timeless agricultural pattern became inevitable once the gospel of Free Trade allowed continental foodstuffs, especially surpluses, to be shipped here. The great social historian Trevelyan wrote: 'The greatest single event of the 'seventies, fraught with immeasurable consequences for the future, was the collapse of agriculture', and this Hardy deeply felt. He realized that much of this was inevitable, in the due process of history and economics: this did not make it less tragic, or its phases and legacies less harsh, and much of value would be forever lost. Thus Hardy's recreation of village life has a strong, often idealized, nostalgia in its detailed perception of a past and cherished way of life. The humblest people, buildings and scenes are made real, factual and alive, and their recreation is informed by and interpreted in situations which are themselves universal.

The limited location of our novel is centred on the village of Puddletown (Hardy's Weatherbury). The place had changed even by the time of his writing the Preface. Puddletown Church can still be seen, however, with its fine Jacobean galleries, a rare Gothic chandelier, and its curious, but beautiful tumbler-shaped Norman font: it contains some fine tombs too. The Great Barn of Chapters 22, 36–7 never existed at Puddletown itself, but there is a fine 15th-century tithe-barn at Abbotsbury, 9 miles (14 km) west of Weymouth (Hardy's Budmouth) which probably served in part, at least, as a model. The old mansion that served as a model for Bathsheba's farm is at Lower Walterstone (or Waterston), formerly the seat of the Martin family, and in the story is a mile or so from its actual position in the valley of the Puddle in the direction of Puddlehinton and Piddletrenthide (Hardy's Lower Longpuddle and Upper Longpuddle respectively).

Most of the action takes place in Weatherbury and its immediate environs, though the movements of a few characters, principally the 'intruders' Bathsheba and Troy, include Bath, Dorchester (Casterbridge) and Weymouth (Budmouth); separate details are offered in the Notes as they appear in the text. For a vivid impression of Dorchester itself one can do little better than to read Hardy's powerful and poignant novel *The Mayor of Casterbridge* (1888).

Detail abounds of the natural setting. A point later to be developed (see 'Structure and style') is how Hardy leaves no doubt as to when things are happening: and the pattern in the book is largely one of Nature's seasonal rhythms and their appropriate agricultural demands. From the physically felt wheel of the stars about Norcombe Hill (Chapter 2) to the flowers around Fanny Robin's coffin and grave (41; 45): from the detail of everyday farming occupations through the cycle of the seasons (lambing, corn-sampling, sheepwashing, tending and shearing, hay-making) to the vivid colours of field and sky at different hours and in varying seasons, we are afforded an artist's view (often in the colours of an artist's palette) of nature's rich fertility, variety and strength. How nature plays a part as an active background to human activity is developed in the section on 'Sympathetic Background'.

Not only do we know what our characters do for their living in their village environment; we are also given details of how they live and think (sometimes so many of their thoughts being revealed that the plot 'creaks' a little). Some, above the common run by their self-education, as Gabriel Oak, are 'not without a frequent consciousness that there was some charm in this life he led' (2,24). Bathsheba likes flowers for their own sake: Boldwood observes with acuteness the play of light on the snow (14,107), and so on. They do not take their surroundings entirely for granted: they can view them, and enjoy them objectively with a sensitive appreciation of their charms.

However, from the conversations of the local farming community – a kind of ballad chorus punctuating the entire story – a great wealth of information can be gathered about the daily, more earthy, thoughts and feelings of the locality: they rarely stand back from the earning of their daily bread for any marvelling at the nature whose whims control and affect their lives so closely. Within their seventeen major interludes (more fully discussed under the section 'Characters') are detailed gossip and superstitions, sharp views on marriage and religion, all of intense local flavour and with a sense of the continuity of things.

Note too that in the pre-railway age (the 'iron horse' did not reach out to Dorchester until Hardy was seven years old) much of the tightness and close-knit complexion of village life was due to this very fact of limited communication. Most people walked: the land-owning farmers had their gigs and carriages, of course;

but the rest used 'shanks's pony', and thus rarely moved out from their native village: and to do so, for any special reason, was a great adventure.

Oak makes his way from Norcombe to Casterbridge – 15 miles (24 km) – considered a 'long way', on foot, before parading himself in the Casterbridge hiring fair, among several hundred similarly unemployed labourers. In all his hundred and seventeen years the ancient Maltster (8) had moved only between Upper Longpuddle, Kingsbere, Norcombe, Durnover, Millpond St Jude's, Mellstock and Weatherbury, all except Norcombe (which is unspecific) within a radius of 5 miles (8 km). Poor Fanny Robin walks her way through the book to her wretched end. Note also how the local time sense is recollected by church holidays and saints' days: however, some of the labourers, especially the younger ones, can write, but most, technically speaking, are illiterate. Nevertheless large portions of the Bible remain in their heads, to be quoted mostly irrelevantly and sometimes irreverently, from their reading and regular church-going, although their adherence is stressed as unthinking and they practise a cosy irreverence when they choose.

There is a great sense of ease, and lack of restlessness, which even the intrusion of Bathsheba and Troy cannot change entirely, among the local community. There is no slacking, to be sure, in the normal course of efficient management, but the pace, the tempo of life is easier and smoother. No one could call Gabriel Oak an easy-going or casual farmer: but he and the others have a rhythm of methodical working which allows for meditation, reminiscence, and a good gossip, the very essence of rural life.

We know that Gabriel Oak can work as his labours demand, from before dawn to the early hours of the next morning, with interrupted sleep thereafter: Bathsheba herself inspects her homestead last thing at night: and historical sources reveal that the usual labourer's wage was under ten shillings a week, although, of course, it was supplemented from his own smallholding and there were always occasional 'perks' of ale and food. Life was always busy, but never rushed; and, indeed, at moments of actual emergency, such as the fire that reunites Oak and Bathsheba (end of Chapter 6) the labourers seem put out of their stride by the sudden pressure.

Overall, and pervading all, is, however, this sense of limited locality and limited worldly experience of a close community. It is the intruders, Bathsheba and Troy, who introduce passion and drama into the calm Weatherbury scene. Bathsheba's parents – the Everdenes – were known 'only a little ... but they were townsfolk': Cain Ball is nearly inarticulate about the virtues of Bath (33); ''Tis for our good to gain knowledge of strange cities', as Poorgrass comments; and Hardy himself significantly comments 'The citizen's *Then* is the rustic's *Now* ... In these Wessex nooks the busy outsider's ancient times are only old; his old times are still new; his present is futurity.' (22,151).

It is against this background, thrust into the family parlours of Victorian England, that this book must be felt and understood.

It is important to notice too that the conversation of the rustic chorus seems authentic in its local dialect, but, in fact, in all their talk, only some thirty-six words or so are actual dialect words not in standard use in the Queen's English. Hardy skilfully conveys the impression of rural life and manners by the matter, the content atmosphere and substance, in the delivery, retort and reaction, rather than by actual style or manner. A glance at any of William Barnes's dialect-poems (a very slight example appears in Chapter 56,390) will indicate the staggering distance between dialect and standard English, and an encounter with a 'Wessex' native who still spoke the local Dorset dialect would leave most of us charmed but largely mystified.

Plot

The plot of *Far from the Madding Crowd* is simple and direct enough. Gabriel Oak first meets Bathsheba Everdene when she enters his village: he falls in love with her, but is rejected. A little later, ruined by the accidental loss of his sheep, he meets her again. She is the new mistress of the farm where he has been taken on as shepherd. The rich neighbour-farmer William Boldwood, encouraged by a valentine sent to him by a capricious Bathsheba, is passionately in love with her. However, he too is rejected in favour of the dashing dragoon sergeant Frank Troy, who wins the flattered Bathsheba as his wife. But Troy has already had an alliance with Fanny Robin, a former ward of Boldwood and later a maidservant at Bathsheba's house: and the abandoned girl and her baby die in the Casterbridge workhouse.

Troy, overcome with remorse, and with his past life exposed, moves off. Thought to have drowned, he returns to Weatherbury as a circus-performer just when Boldwood seems certain of marrying the apparently widowed Bathsheba. In a dramatic scene Boldwood shoots Troy when he demands the return of his wife. Troy is killed: Boldwood is imprisoned for life as a lunatic, and the patient, devoted, dogged Oak, finally marries the sadder and wiser Bathsheba.

It will soon be noticed by the attentive reader that Hardy's plot 'creaks' somewhat. There are many places where chance and coincidence seem to have an exaggeratedly long arm. In sequence, for example, there are Oak's wagon-ride to where he wishes to go (6) and its consequences; the 'Troubles in the Fold' so soon after Oak's dismissal (21); Troy's arrival in the story at that particular juncture (24); the revel coinciding with the storm (36–8); Fanny's meeting Troy and Bathsheba (39); the gurgoyle's conspiracy with the weather directed at Fanny's grave and Troy's handiwork there (46); his rescue from drowning (47) and his eventual return just at the time of the Greenhill Fair (50); Pennyways' presence there and elsewhere (23) after his dismissal; and the whole episode of Troy's stealing the revealing note (50): and there are other coincidences less pronounced. Again, Hardy reveals much of his plot by direct statement, exposing the machinery of his construction, as it were, and not allowing his characters to take on the full weight of the movement of the story by themselves. This feature was commented on further in the section 'Characters'.

It must be stated here, and it will again be emphasized, that Hardy believed in such chance and coincidence: none of this is impossible in life itself, given the situations and characters involved in and developed through the plot. He re-echoes Hamlet's notion that 'There's a divinity that shapes our ends, Rough-hew them how we will.'

This is the way the world goes, in all its shortcomings, cruelty and injustice. Thus the plot may well be commonplace and humdrum, but it is Hardy's view of a typical slice of pastoral life.

Much of the plot's 'staginess' and its occasional touch of melodrama is conditioned by the necessity of serial-unity, for this demands an evenly spaced sequence of sensational climaxes. The plot is only a structure, after all, which comes to life with the flesh and blood of its characters. Many of Shakespeare's plots, for example, if barely stated and baldly summarized, are poor, and some even absurd. But the language, the poetry, the creativeness add the richness we remember. Here too, the five suffering characters playing out life's ironies are richly and sensitively drawn, in a particular atmosphere, with great sympathy and skill. Structurally the plot is extremely tight and controlled.

Sympathetic background

A phrase of Ruskin's in his *Modern Painters* (1843–60) condemned the crediting of Nature with human emotion: 'All violent feelings ... produce ... a falseness in ... impressions of external things, which I would generally characterize as the "pathetic fallacy".' This was directed principally at 'Romantic' art: but literature too abounds with examples where natural objects are endowed with human emotions, so that there seems some correspondence and coincidence between Nature and humanity. It can of course, be overplayed: but in great literature Nature often symbolically shares and enhances the heightened moments of human emotion, projecting a limited human situation into universal significance. It is almost commonplace in the great tragedies of Shakespeare, the Odes of Keats and the poems of Wordsworth: storms, mists, tempests, nightfall, winds, clouds, flowers and bird-song (to take only some more obvious examples) are used as symbols, enlarging the human situation into a timeless universal experience.

Hardy's use of this sympathetic background may often be more melodramatic; certainly, in later, darker works he developed the technique so that inanimate features, such as Egdon Heath, take on a breathing, powerful, inexorable will of their own: but even in this early novel there are clear indications of his firm grasp of the potentialities of this treatment of a sympathetic bond between humankind and the universe, the relentless detached cosmos. It is possible, one must be warned, to read too much into such sequences, or even to attach a symbolism to scenes which they cannot properly bear. Nevertheless there are certain points in the development of the story where this sympathetic background seems to come into full play, and not to realize it may limit one's approach to the text.

The opening paragraphs of Chapter 2 suggest a permanence humanly embodied in Oak himself, and the 'stately progress' of the earth is compared with his own 'special power' of 'quiet energy': there is, too, the obvious large contrast of the spinning cosmos of the universe, the quiet movements of Gabriel, and the helpless gestures of the new-born lambs into this dark world.

Incidentally, it is noteworthy how often Hardy expresses sympathy for the dumb creatures of his natural backgrounds (e.g. 'Many a small bird went to bed supperless that night among the bare boughs': 3,31; the details given of his sheepdogs, especially in 5; the afflicted sheep of 21 and the employment of Old Pleasant in 41). All Hardy's twilight scenes are noteworthy in their associations with their human watchers: the dawn reveals, exposes, challenges (3, 5, 9, and especially the end of 14, 25, 38, 40, and the opening of 44); evenings usually darken in some dramatic, pathetic or tragic note.

Of greater and more symbolic importance, however, are such scenes as that of the opening of Chapter 11, where the nightfall, the drabness, the cold, the muffled bell, the small shape of the slight girl against the great masses of the wall, sky and river, even the weakness of her aim, all unite to emphasize a nullity, a negation, a hopelessness and despair, against which the assertions of the soldier on one side of the window and impenetrable wall, unseen and just heard, seem themselves ominously negative and unpromising.

The very seasons of the year are significant for the triangle of lovers: Oak is rejected in January; late spring gives hope to Boldwood; and early summer sees Boldwood's passion flooding, and Troy's chance intrusion, which ripens as summer passes, reaching fruition with his marriage to Bathsheba in the middle of July; Fanny dies as the autumn yields to winter, and Troy is killed as the year itself dies, Bathsheba reviving as the New Year progresses, her hopes of reconciliation with Oak waning as the year quietly passes, until her desperate intervention in 56.

The sheep-shearing scene of Chapter 22 abounds in 'sympathetic' colouring: the rich potential of the landscape, the historic background of the church-like barn, Hardy's philosophical asides, even the colouring of the shorn sheepskin and its comparison to Aphrodite significantly re-echo the waning aspirations of Gabriel, the increasing attentions of Boldwood, the notions of marriage bandied about by the labourers, all centred on the lady in their midst. Troy enters in darkness, ominously (24): and 28 is worth special attention, for it is crucial. The atmosphere is isolated, yet lush: the sword-play brilliant yet dangerous: every detail has a significance beyond the words employed, as has already been seen.

The storm scene of Chapters 36–8 is highly charged in its

symbolism. Oak, the silent resigned lover separated from his love and the atmosphere of revelling imposed by Troy, his successful and flashy rival, reads all the portents, and once again is the sole saviour of Bathsheba's wealth, which Troy recklessly squanders. He works alone and dangerously, and then side by side with Bathsheba, who knows what he feels, throughout the dramatic ominous lightning-storm. The flashes reveal the blinding truth of Bathsheba's moral predicament and feminine caprice, but the bonds between her and Oak are silently made stronger and more durable as the thatch grows over the naked ricks.

And then the two hapless lovers, Oak and Boldwood, meet in the rain: one, at great personal risk, having maintained his integrity and showed his worth despite the apparently immovable impediment of Bathsheba's foolhardy marriage, the other so obsessed with his loss on the same grounds, that he has neglected his own livelihood and is careless even of his own life. This is a powerfully written and carefully balanced scene, which deserves careful rereading.

Other examples abound. Chapter 40 contains some examples of one of Hardy's favourite interests, that of the interplay of light and shade: and there is the funeral note of the fox's bark, the friendly dog which has to be stoned off, and the ivy-clad workhouse. A melancholy shrouding mist surrounds Joseph and his pathetic burden (42), and Bathsheba's return to 'The Hollow amid the Ferns' (44) is significant. This was the scene of Troy's first amorous display and Bathsheba's first kiss: now it is a retreat, a desperate escape from his presence.

Note too how the 'rescuing' Liddy has to cross a swamp to the now-dismal spot. While normal life for Bathsheba has temporarily stopped, and she undergoes voluntary self-imprisonment, note how the sun sets (44); the young men released from labour play Prisoners' base, only to leave their sport to see Fanny's tombstone. Nature again despoils Fanny's grave after Troy's extravagant remorse (46); and night shrouds all Troy's sinister manoeuvres, his murder, and Boldwood's self-surrender to the law: it is late at night when his commuted sentence is announced.

Structure and style

Structure

The plot of *Far from the Madding Crowd* being so straightforward, one can easily miss the niceties of its structure. It has already been mentioned that the plot 'creaks' somewhat for various reasons. However Hardy had to compose his story in serial form, and this involved a very close grasp of structural techniques. Readers expected a spacing of major events; definite climaxes, and moments of suspense; progression had to be clear, without obvious gulfs; characters had to be carefully introduced, and consistent; material should not be made to stretch, as it were, artificially, and so on. The exact limits of each monthly part were as follows, from January 1874 until November 1874; Chapters 1–5; 6–8; 9–14; 15–19; 20–4; 25–9; 30–3; 34–8; 39–42; 43–7; 48–57. To indicate and emphasize this the revision questions in these Notes are arranged to fall at these intervals.

The attentive reader will see how neatly and cleverly this division, despite the drawbacks of serialization, assists the movement of the story. A careful reading of the closing paragraph of one part, and the opening of the next will confirm it without details being provided here. The serialization, indeed, gives the story a perceptible rhythm, a pulse, and a clear direction.

Complementary to this is Hardy's chronological accuracy. The entire tale is set in a pastoral background: nature looms large; and this very setting controls the story as much as it does the lives and livelihoods of the community. The serial started in January 1874; the novel starts on a morning in December (the year, though this is unimportant, can be calculated as being 1870, for we are told that 13 February is a Sunday). The careful reader is aware, and Hardy's original readership buying the instalments month by month would be closely aware, of the fact that Hardy provides an abundance of dates; months, days, and even hours are carefully inserted as the novel progresses. The openings of many serial parts, for example, are usually explicit briefly and immediately, in their time relations: 'Two months passed away' (6); 'by daylight . . .' (9); 'Half an hour later . . .' (3);

'That same evening . . .' (34), and so on.

The agricultural year, with its seasonable occupations, is followed through rigorously: interestingly enough, up to the last instalment (48–57 of November 1874) the chapter groupings correspond to the actual month of the year in which they appeared, sometimes a little in arrear, sometimes a little in advance: but they are always close enough to be familiar and actual by merely looking out of one's window. The last instalment of course runs through the whole nine months of Bathsheba's widowhood, and by moving into the autumn marks up the second year of the whole story. A patiently constructed time-chart would convince the reader of this formal accuracy of Hardy's dating and timing, and would reveal how it gives coherence, shape and a certain tightness to the whole unwinding plot. There is never any possible doubt when (or for that matter, where) any event takes place.

This external framework is reinforced from within, with great deftness, by many situations, shedding light on the characters and episodes of the story itself. Intervals for time are needed to space out both characters and events. Thus, for example, we have gaps between Gabriel's loss of his sheep and his re-encounter with Bathsheba; the filled in detail of Fanny Robin's long marches and frustrations; Troy's interval of leave with all its consequences; Bathsheba's pursuit of Troy, his long absence, and his fateful return. All this time other strands of the story are being extended, completed or merged with other material. And often there are references which are peculiarly prophetic, time being the constant ally of chance and fate.

Consider, as a detail, the conversation between Bathsheba and Oak at his proposal (4). Examine the list of things Oak suggests, and note how these in fact appear later on. The piano; one of the first things the newly independent Bathsheba installs, yet talked about as a typically 'high-falutin' and pretentious possession in the village; the reference to 'gentleman and lady' foreshadows the introduction of the only formal 'gentleman', socially, of the story, Farmer Boldwood, and Bathsheba would dearly like to be known as a 'lady' of the community. The newspaper announcement of a marriage certainly appears, ironically, at a dreadful moment when the 'trickster' Troy, playing a cat-and-mouse with Boldwood's fevered emotions, shows him the dreaded news. And the babies: well, none is to come to

Bathsheba, but one does to Fanny Robin, unfolding tremendous consequences.

Whatever the faults of Hardy's style, however much we may regret his dependence on what seems to us wild chance and coincidence, few errors can be noted in his painstaking construction. Here there is great strength, a firm grip on the movement, a careful progression and swing towards the end in view. It is a merit easily unrecognized, for it is of 'the art which conceals art'.

Style

The text of *Far from the Madding Crowd* is that of a long novel, in a particular setting with many-sided characters, by an author still young in the art of composition and yet intent on posing and handling particular problems and emotions in a distinctive way. It would be foolish, and even dangerous, to attempt any simple analysis of Hardy's style, or to base a general estimate on any one single aspect or part of the whole story. Sooner or later, one must get down to fundamental elements, even down to the words themselves, before one can assume a unified view of the style of the entire story.

It may be best to consider first some of Hardy's weaknesses. To begin with, his style is *allusive*. At a conservative count, there are over forty references to the Bible, some quite obscure; about thirty to Greek and Latin allusions, and an equal number to other literary quotations or figures; over twenty to scientific and astronomical terms; eleven to names of artists; a few (surprisingly few, considering Hardy's background) to architecture; a number of references to music, history, flowers, and a few to birds (again surprisingly few for an observant countryman). It is of course true that the educated novel reading public of the time would not be unduly put out by this: Hardy's own characters quote the Bible readily and naturally (e.g. the labourers in Chapter 8, Maryann the cleaning-woman in Chapter 9).

Nevertheless some examples of his allusions are extreme even for the well-educated. The inclusion of such references as eight heads, Saint-Simon, Chain Salpae, mathematical sections of a cone, St John Long, Chromis and Mnasylus, an obscure maxim of Hippocrates, and a Greek word in the original are unduly heavy, for they have been made part and parcel of the narrative, and send one scuttling to reference books (not necessarily a bad thing, of course) to elucidate the author's meaning. Some of this seems a little like a display of knowledge for its own sake, found often in the self-educated unsure writer striving to prove his intellectual background.

In the same way, there is often *verbosity* and *redundance*, with ponderous words, clumsily polysyllabic, and unhappy phrases, which a little patience could have ironed out into smoother simpler writing: a random sample can include such words as perpendicularity, impassibleness, firmamental, tergiversation, factitious, plethora, and a number of pieces are rather unpolished and approach jargon.

We have already noted that, in places, the mechanism of the novel is clumsy: the plot creaks with occasional stretches of coincidence, there are touches of melodrama, and constant climaxes, a great deal of this consequent upon its serial construction. Again, Hardy reveals, from his own viewpoint, much of the stream of personality, not always allowing his characters to reveal themselves: this often deepens the story without advancing it. Long passages of objective writing hold up (not necessarily 'padding out') the movement (e.g. 1, 1; most of 12, 18, 25): and some of this becomes a little dull and stiff. One waits a little anxiously for the next plain statement that will set the imagination working again and the tale to continue.

Not to mention this debit side is to be uncritical: to over-emphasize it would be even more unsound. For Hardy never pretends to be a master of language (or of anything, indeed, in his natural quiet modesty). The virtues of his style far outweigh these flaws, which have, of course, been carefully and deliberately extracted. These may well present, as Blunden wrote, 'remarkable spasms of contorted and straggling English' and reveal 'inartistic knottiness', but over its entire range, it is a strikingly direct and forceful style, of great pressure and versatility.

First, one must note its *visual exactness* based on keen observation and a painter's talent for colour, detail and impression, particularly of sharply contrasting shades and overall atmosphere. The panoramic landscapes and 'sky-scapes' of many chapters (especially the openings of 2, 8, 9, 11, 15, 28, 32, 35), are lovingly and sharply drawn: visual reality is blended with a poetic lustre, which touches off the imagination. The detail of colour (e.g. crimson, ochreous, amaranthine, chinchilla, rich Indian red) is exact and rich.

Then there is the internal pressure of *pace and rhythm*, suited to the movement of a particular scene or situation. A close inspection of the prose will reveal Hardy's skill here, in presentation both of scenery and character. Chapter 2, 20–21: 'The hill ... heard no more' is a good but not untypical example. Description and atmosphere blend. Shapes are distinct (arched curve, crowning boughs); sounds are reinforced by onomatopoeia and alliteration. The verbs have an exact force (smote, floundered, simmered and boiled, rattled, raking): key words are so placed as to take the stress (tonight, keenest, gushed, sob, plunged, etc.). The variation of sentence length, and therefore of the retention of the thought within each varying sentence, builds up into a set of sound-climaxes, pushed out finally by the force of 'the hurrying gust', and sighing away on the open vowels of 'to be heard no more'. Deliberate or not – and examples could be multiplied endlessly – this is evocative and powerful writing. In moments of crisis, climatic, physical or moral the rhythm takes on by cumulative effect a strong lifting grandeur, giving the total story an internal pulse of the large rhythms of a ballad tale.

It may be applying too 'scientific' an approach to a literary form, but it is at least interesting to note how the story does in fact pivot about the central chapter (29); and at regular intervals on either side of this the pressures, lesser and greater, are applied. It is instructive to mark these off on the contents pages once one is thoroughly conversant with the text. Note the balancing of 28 and 30 on either side of the centre, then, moving outwards, the parallel nature of, say 22–3 and 36–7, 16 and 44, 7, the first view of Fanny Robin and 53, the final consequences of her ever having lived. By such design or other, there is a strong sense of balances and weighs, point and counterpoint, pulsating through the story.

Hardy's skill in 'placing' is clearly shown in his dialogue and 'dialect'. The conversations run naturally and smoothly, well in character; and the 'dialect' gives the strongest impression of rustic talk in substance and style, though not in actual language. There are many interesting encounters in speech, which go far in emphasizing or elaborating a character: Bathsheba, for example, varies her tone and attitude considerably according to her audience, be it Oak, Boldwood, her farmhands, or Liddy; and with Troy there is a delightful blend of defensiveness and weakness (26–8). Boldwood's conversations vary too in pitch

with Bathsheba, Oak or Troy. In general, they skilfully change
in weight, direction, poise and social distance.

There is great *emotional force* in Hardy's writing, one which
often gives it a height and a grandeur associated with poetry.
This can range from stark scenes, almost like those of classical
tragedy, such as between Bathsheba and Boldwood (31) or of
Troy's death (end of 53), to the lyrical feeling underlying most
of the landscapes and of 28. There is, too, the haunting nostalgia
of such passages as Boldwood's meditations (14–15), the description of Great Barn (22), and some superb flights of imagery in
the views of the stars and the feel of the wheeling universe (2),
and in the great storm scene (37).

Nor are these examples in any way exhaustive. This emotional
and poetic force is often allied in Hardy to the macabre, the
strikingly odd, the grotesque. This is revealed, for example, in
the moments of Boldwood's brooding passions, the first outside
view of the malthouse, the detail of the fir plantation, the storm,
the opening of Fanny's coffin, and the gurgoyle's overflow.
These, and many of the night scenes, are drawn with a touch of
that haunting sinister dread of a child's recollections of terror,
with great visual exactness and vividness. This is a 'Gothic' touch
(like that often satirized in Jane Austen's novels), and appears
also in Hardy's soaring descriptions of vast sky expanses, of lofty
buildings, of shades and shadows.

With this general survey in mind, it is instructive to inspect
closely a complete chapter, to note Hardy at work. Chapter 28
offers a typical sample of his imaginative and descriptive
powers. Time and place are made clear at once: as is the colour
of the dying day on the foliage. Bathsheba's emotions are made
equally clear: the ferns 'caress' her. She is excited, trembling and
panting, wondering what is to befall, yet eager to experience it.
Her eyes shine: she is losing herself; and Troy is there, looking
up from the hollow. Note the effect and placing of the sunshine,
and the plush nature of the mossy earth. The whole setting is
soft, secret, lush, promising.

Then follows the brilliant sword-play (pp.189–91) with its
physical implications. Troy is quiet, controlled, methodical,
practised: the whole atmosphere is charged and meteoric. All
the senses are appealed to – vividly, excitingly. Then Troy snips
off the lock of hair, and splits a caterpillar on her bodice, and on
the frightening revelation that the sword was razor-sharp, Troy

slips it back to safety into the scabbard. He has won: Bathsheba is quite overcome, and in her defeat, he kisses her, sealing the emotional crisis. Note the technique of 'placing' throughout: the general scene, moving to a particular setting, and then viewed from different angles. Troy goes, disappearing like a magic wave from his own sword, and then we are told of his embrace and its consequences.

Although there is little variation in the 'verbs of saying' in the conversation, usually a weakness, with eleven examples of the neutral 'said' and only two changes ('interrupted' and 'cried'), the dialogue runs smoothly, dramatic in form by omission of introductory words very often, and changing in tone and attitude appropriate to the situation. Accuracy is sharp: the adjectives have strength; there is inner movement and pace, governed by the length and pauses of the sentence. There is no elaboration or decoration: it is all fresh and unforced, the sequences clear and unfolding naturally, with the climax almost silent yet powerful. The atmosphere and colouring are matched to the circumstances, and over all there is a magical, poetic, creative impression and inspiration, hard to analyse in its kinship to poetry. That is to be felt again in many places: in Fanny's wanderings and death, in Troy's Romanticism' and in the gurgoyle episode, and others.

Exploration of *figurative language* is always profitable: with Hardy it ranges from the commonplace and near-prosaic (e.g. 'flew in clusters like birds from a nest' and 'silent as a tomb') to concrete and sharply visual similes such as 'arched curve . . . like a mane', 'like the coal of a cigar', a tooth 'like a milestone in a bank' to the rural and proverbial 'a temper mild as milk' and (of a beard) 'like the grey moss and lichen upon a leafless apple-tree'. Every page yields a crop of such living similes, and rich metaphors also abound. Many are of light: 'light raking the earth', 'garnish light of mockery', 'green shadows'; and much of the landscapes are in fact extended metaphors, sometimes with blended images (technically called 'synaesthesia') like those of the lightning (37), 'The flash . . . dance of death'. Devices such as *assonance, alliteration*, and *onomatopoeia*, common enough in lyrical poetry, are often used on the soaring imaginative flights of heightened emotions: e.g. Boldwood ruminating on the frost (14); the rain soaking Gabriel (38), the dawn view of the swamp (44). The figurative language shows sharp focus and vivid arresting precision.

It is interesting to note that, although this is a novel of human passions and of the irony of fate, one is left with a sense of joy. Partly, of course, this is because the foolish have been punished and the wicked destroyed: although innocents suffer too, and Bathsheba herself, for one so capricious, gets off rather lightly. But in a greater measure it is Hardy's sympathy, to man and beast, which is satisfying: and, of course, the humour of the local community is remembered. Much of the book is ironical, some is cynical; but a sense of freshness and positive happiness is preserved, without recourse to actual open humour among the major characters. The pastoral scenes, the natural unchanging settings, the beauties of nature and the essential goodness of such people as Oak and Fanny contribute to this wholesome spirit.

There is a grandeur, in fact, about Hardy's total work. Clumsy undoubtedly in minor patches, the writing is yet creative, especially on the large high splendours of land, sky and the smouldering emotions of humankind. The narrative is bold and purposeful; details are accurate; and there is a weight, a steady pressure of feeling behind it all. The language sometimes seems ungainly, but the total effect is sure enough, and it may be disturbing by intention. Hardy himself, rather disarmingly, had his own answer to those who accused him of a 'general attack upon language'. As he said: 'The secret of a living style lies in not having too much style – in being a little careless, or sounding to be, here and there ...' An acute realism, the frequent biblical cadence, a latent poetry, the long held contemplation of natural scenic beauty, and a sinewy rich turn of word and phrase give Hardy's style a durability. It is not always sustained and it is not easily definable: but here is a great, often a rugged strength, a coherence and clarity, touched with a timeless grandeur evolved from and surely provoked by the Wessex countryside whose tales he wished to tell.

General questions plus questions on related topics for coursework/examinations on other books you may be studying

1 Trace the development of Boldwood's growing mental instability.

Suggested notes for essay answer:

1 Scope and initial procedure.

The sad and eventually tragic story of Boldwood is actively pursued through its peaks and troughs of remoteness, uncertainty, expectation, happiness and bleak despair in twenty-three of the novel's fifty-seven chapters (with other occasional passing references). Close study and careful note-taking from the text are essential to isolate the relevant material: appropriate quotations should be listed.

NB The question does not demand a character sketch, but rather evidences of a characteristic, a trait of personality, an obsession which develops. Those strands which suggest Boldwood's instability must therefore be separated from the overall text. They will comprise his own actions, reactions and words, his reported thoughts, other characters' comments and opinions as the story develops, and include Hardy's own viewpoints.

2 Technique.

Extract key references in sequence, briefly noting their context. The details are carefully interwoven from Chapter 9 onwards, usually in compact groups (Chapters 9–10; 12–19; 22–24; 30–31; 34, 38, 41; 49–53; 55).

3 Suggestions and examples (mixture of quotations and comment).

(a) Early hints:

Chapter 9 – stern-looking, hopeless man for a woman

12 – wrapt up and indifferent, distant, possibly once jilted

14 – whole chapter needs careful reading: nervous excitability, listlessness

15 – constrained, restless countenance

17 – women as remote phenomena

18 – isolated in Weatherby society, not an ordinary

nature, equilibrium disturbed, he was in extremity at once.

(b) Developments:

    18 – whole paragraph: 'The phases of Boldwood's life . . . or he was missed', and the next 'He had no light . . . to end tragically'.

       Later: '. . . now living outside his defences . . . when they love': look too at last paragraph.

    19 – Declaration of his love and proposal, opening of sluices of feeling: re-read carefully the whole conversation, and note the last paragraph.

(c) Effect of Troy's intervention:

    24 – last sentence

    30 – letter to Boldwood

    31 – its consequences: note Chapter title 'Blame-Fury', and Boldwood's prophetic threats – fevered feeling, loss of self-mastery.

(d) Continuation (summarized):

further crucial elements added as story proceeds e.g. (especially) in Chapter 34 – interestingly enough the only time when Boldwood's Christian name (William) is stated in self-identification. Here he is dealing with a heartless trickster: there are threats of murder, and note the final sentence-paragraph. Hereafter the Chapters indicated in Section 2 above emphasize Boldwood's decline: abandoning his farm duties (38), his pursuit of Bathsheba after Troy's (apparent) death by drowning, and the tentative promise of marriage. The pace hastens with the long Chapter 52 (note the title, and the final paragraph of Part VI). Chapter 53, with its rising tempo, is also significant to the theme. Note how Boldwood 'compresses' his emotions, and the long conversation with Bathsheba: look at the words – eagerly, blissful loving intimacy, husky voice, 'I would give up my life for you', his being absorbed in visions. There follows his transformation into 'sudden despair' and the murder of Troy, and his attempt at suicide. Chapter 55 details the symptoms of mental derangement in his packed and dated collection of clothes and jewellery: the stern, dignified, but haunted man once of iron self-control had passed over the brink – the razor's edge that divides the sane from the insane mind.

2 Which descriptive parts of the novel appeal to you most, and why?

3 Does the long arm of coincidence stretch too far or too obviously anywhere in the story?

4 Indicate five or six examples of Hardy's interest in and close perception of the contrasts of light and shade.

5 Give examples of Hardy's familiarity with and knowledge of painting, literature, music and the Bible.

6 What episodes do you associate with Yalbury Hill, the Buck's Head Inn, the Great Barn, Lulwind Cove, Greenhill?

7 It has been said that Bathsheba shows more character than personality. What do you think is meant by this?

8 Why does Bathsheba open Fanny Robin's coffin? Trace the situation leading up to this, and summarize the principal consequences of her action.

9 Write a character sketch of Gabriel Oak. Does he change at all during the story?

10 Describe Gabriel's first courtship of Bathsheba.

11 Compare and contrast Boldwood and Troy.

12 In what ways is Troy likeable?

13 Comment on the individuality of the 'rustic chorus'.

14 Describe the scene of Troy's death: what makes it vivid?

15 'Hardy's men . . . are inadequate as human beings, and even more inadequate as fictional creations.' Discuss.

16 What humour have you found in the novel?

17 Show how irony and cynicism run through the story.

18 What, in your opinion, are the principal defects and virtues of Hardy's style?

19 'Not a powerful analyst of human life, but a meditative story-teller or romancer.' Comment closely on this impression as it applies to this novel.

20 Do you find Hardy's view of life tragic or pessimistic?

Additional coursework questions

1 Give a brief account of any novel you have read which is set almost entirely in the countryside of England or the USA.

2 Describe a humorous incident in an otherwise sad or tragic story.

3 Show how a writer has developed the theme of jealousy in a book or play you have studied.

4 Describe how and why a character in one of your books has unexpectedly reappeared after a long period of absence, and explain the consequences of his or her reappearance.

5 From your reading describe in some detail an incident (and its after-effects) of a fire, thunderstorm, hurricane or other violent natural disaster.

6 Describe a character in a book you have studied who yields to temptation: indicate, briefly, the consequences.

7 Indicate the parts played by any two or three minor characters in a play or novel familiar to you.

8 From one or two books you have read show the effects of an 'outsider' joining or trying to join a small group, or of larger numbers of 'outsiders' trying to integrate into a section of society.

9 Some people claim that 'A woman's place is in the home: it's a man's world'. From your reading (fact or fiction) show that one or two writers have opposed such a view.

10 From one or two books you have read or studied describe the consequences, on the partners or their children, of the breakdown of a marriage.

Further reading

Earlier 'standard' books remain useful for general reading: use the Contents page and/or the Index.

Life of Thomas Hardy, Mrs F. E. Hardy (Macmillan)

Thomas Hardy, Edmund Blunden (Macmillan)

Hardy the Novelist, Lord David Cecil (Constable)

The Young Thomas Hardy, Robert Gittings (Heinemann Educational, Penguin)

The Older Thomas Hardy, Robert Gittings (Heinemann Educational)

Among many other more recent works, the following are recommended:

A Hardy Companion, F. B. Pinion (Macmillan, 1968)

The Life and Work of Thomas Hardy, Michael Millgate (Macmillan, 1985)

How to Study a Hardy Novel, John Peck (Macmillan, 1987)

A Thomas Hardy Dictionary, F. B. Pinion (Macmillan, 1990)